Healthy Indian Recipes—
Ultimate Cooking Guide

Healthy Indian Recipes— Ultimate Cooking Guide

Healthy approach to Indian cooking

This book supports Children's Charity—Mary's Meals!
All information available at the back of this book

H. Karam Ellahie

To order additional copies of this book, contact:
Xlibris Corporation
0-800-644-6988
www.xlibrispublishing.co.uk
Orders@xlibrispublishing.co.uk
303781

Contents

Over 100 Indian recipes for snacks, curries, rice dishes, Indian breads, condiments, desserts and beverages. These are flavoursome, authentic, easy, wholesome and economical recipes with some beneficial food facts and realistic cooking tips—all in one book.

H. Karam Ellahie

Foreword

Hameeda has lived in the United Kingdom for many years but still remembers and honours the cuisine of India. She is a faithful and enthusiastic Christian who has long been a member of the United Benefice of St Paul's and St Mary's in Surrey and often arrives at church events and Bible Study groups with wonderful aromatic dishes.

A gifted and experienced science teacher as well as an expert cook, Hameeda works hard to harmonise traditional Indian recipes with ingredients easily available over here and thinks carefully about what is most appropriate to the occasion and the friends, family or larger church groups to be fed. She has made lamb dishes and the unleavened bread for our Maundy Thursday celebration of the Last Supper, as well as samosas and pakoras for fellowship meals and parties. All she does is offered with love and prayer, a sense of tradition and an awareness of what is good and healthy for both body and soul!

I have much pleasure in commending her book, 'Healthy Indian recipes –Ultimate cooking guide' and look forward to trying the recipes myself.

Rev. C. Bourne

Appreciations and Recommendations of the author's cooking . . .

I have known Hameeda as a very dear friend for over 30 years and we have enjoyed exchanging western, Punjabi and Guajarati recipes with each other. My late husband was very fond of her rice pulaos, aloo parathas and all her curries. My son loved her koffata kebabs. Fish biryani, fresh fruit chickpea chaart, pakoras and zarda rice with pineapple (Sweet yellow rice) are my favourites among many other of her dishes that I have enjoyed. I strongly recommend her recipes, they are worth trying!

N. Jiwaji

Hameeda has kindly shared several of her delicious home-cooked dishes with our family over the years. She has a large repertoire of family recipes for starters, main meals and desserts. They contain a wide variety of healthy, natural ingredients which blend together to produce fragrant aromas and many interesting flavours.

V. Shingles

I am looking forward to buying Hameeda's cookery book. Her Indian cooking I have sampled at our International Food Festival is so good, that I only wish she held a master class.

J. Phillips

I have known Hameeda for many years. Her cooking is not only good for you nutritionally but it is delicious. It has inspired me to try some of her curry recipes and they were a success. I pray that her expertise will do the same for you.

J. Jones

I have been the grateful and enthusiastic recipient of Hameeda's Indian starters and curries and each time it has been a delight. Authentic cooking from someone in the know that never fails to satisfy. I look forward to buying a copy and getting stuck in!

M. Chambers

Her delicately-flavoured samosas, pakoras, tuna fish and potato kebabs, chickpea and fresh fruit chaart (salad), raitas, vegetable curry, daal and bean curry, meatball curry, lamb curry and chicken curry with chickpea/ pea rice pulao are the highlights of the many international charity suppers held at Church.

C. Shearer

Really enjoyed the food cooked by Hameeda. Authentic Indian cuisines cooked by someone from India/Pakistan, but with Hameeda's own blend of inventiveness.

L. Randall

I always looked forward to the Indian meals that Hameeda happily cooked and brought to work; they were always very tasty and full of flavour. I would fully recommend that her recipes be tried and be tasted by all who enjoy Indian food. Pakoras, meatball curry, chicken/lamb curry and the chicken rice pulao with the Indian condiments were the best for me.

A. Gregory

I have cooked, eaten and fed other people using Hameeda's easy and workable recipes and everyone I know who has eaten that food, found it amazingly delicious. I have eaten in Indian restaurants all over the world and have yet to find anything that tastes so good.

A. Muammar

Hameeda's food was always very flavoursome *but I especially remember her pakoras as being the best I had tasted then or ever since! I have never eaten any better pakoras. Now, every time that I eat one I always think back to her and her pakoras.* Everyone always looked forward to her bringing in meals and could not get enough of her tasty food.

D. Dobbs

Carrot, potato and peas curry, using Hameeda's recipe, won many compliments at a curry party for over twenty people.

C. Shearer

When Hameeda worked with me her Indian lunches were eagerly anticipated by all of us and lived up to everyone's expectations—all recipes available and highly recommended, try them for yourself!

P. Hodson

All the great variety of homemade Indian food that Hameeda generously cooked for her colleagues has always been absolutely fantastic, much better than anything bought from a restaurant! The meatball curry, chicken pulao rice, tandoori chicken and black eye bean curry were particularly favourites of mine.

M. Curtis

I found Hameeda's cooking to be absolutely delicious! The combinations of ingredients were very attractive and colourful and the food was very well spiced.

A. Webb

I have tried a few of Hameeda's recipes and have found them easy to follow and very tasty. My favourite dish is her minced beef and potato curry and I look forward to trying out some new tasty dishes from her recipe book.

J. Tonks

'Healthy Indian recipes –Ultimate cooking guide' offers simple honest recipes which no doubt you will enjoy. I have tasted Hameeda's delicious meat/vegetable curries, pulaos, pakoras and many more dishes. Therefore I can thoroughly recommend you to give it a try!

M. Haffner

I am very fond of her cooking because it is not all about chilli-hot food but everything is delicately flavoured. Hameeda's recipes are not only nutritious and balanced but without excessive use of salt, sugar and fat.

H. Farrukh

Acknowledgement

I am grateful to my sons for appreciating all my efforts which go in the preparation of the food cooked for them. They now realise that the time is approaching when they need to consider learning some of the Indian dishes they really enjoy. So they requested that I write all the recipes for the food I cook. I loved the idea and started writing exactly what and how I do my cooking. This was appealing to me and then on the serious note I thought it is a good opportunity to document a simple guide to my recipes in a proper manner. At that stage I didn't realise that I was taking on the challenge of producing a cookery book. Almost a year ago I experienced a similar situation; started writing short prayers to be shared with others. But by the God given passion, determination, inspiration and by the encouragement of family and friends it turned into a prayer book, 'Catalysts for your prayers'.

It was published in February 2012, to bless the souls of many. If interested please read the seven pages of excerpt from the book, on amazon.co.uk to sample the book. But this time I felt the urgency to encourage and to give full support to people, to learn and to succeed in cooking healthy Indian food. I consider that I fully dedicated myself in this service to **everyone,** by creating 'Healthy Indian recipes –Ultimate cooking guide'.

Almost thirty-nine years ago; I got married and came to live in England. I was coming from a background where most of the food was prepared for me. However, when I had to do all my own cooking I faced it courageously and focused on learning, experimenting and improving the art of simple and healthy cooking. It was remarkable that very soon I was able not only to cook food of a good standard but also able to encourage and to teach others as well. I am truly thankful to all my relatives, friends, neighbours and colleagues who genuinely accepted and enjoyed whatever was cooked for them. I am humbled by all the appreciations and the recommendations of my cooking (some of the comments are added to the book—see p15-17). These comments gave me great encouragement and confidence to create a book on healthy Indian cooking.

I dedicate this book to my son Samuel and Paul, to the future generations and *to all those who are lovers of Indian food and are eager to learn Indian cooking.*

H. Karam Ellahie

Introduction

Besides cooking food every day for my family, I am privileged to have cooked for my sons' school fun fairs, for the local Church's Christmas/Summer fairs and fundraising events for the charities. My Indian cooking had always gone very well for the international suppers held by St. Pauls Church. This successful and enjoyable event for the community has raised money for several charities and this year (Feb.2013) Mary's Meal will be one of them. Wherever I have worked I had always been generous to share the authentic taste of Indian cooking with all my colleagues; which was always appreciated. Most of the gifts to my friends have been my humble and simple homemade Indian food, which is always happily accepted and enjoyed. *Through the above mentioned occasions, I have kept the taste of the Indian food alive. Although it is hard work, it gives me an opportunity to put my recipes to the test and a chance to improve my cooking, too.*

What is the aim of 'Healthy Indian recipes –Ultimate cooking guide'?

Homemade food is always economical, tastier, safer and free from processed ingredients and artificial-preservatives, flavours and colourings, when compared with some of the fast foods and some pre-prepared meals. Nevertheless, we can't deny that these convenient alternatives of readymade meals are there for us when we are stuck for time to cook.

Home-produced food is also a 'green product' as there is no wastage on packaging and no disposal of the packaging means reduction in environmental pollution.

Cooking is an art and a discipline and needs to be acquired by learning, by application and by practice. Therefore I have personally made every effort to write these simple recipes with great clarity in the confidence that this discipline will be achieved by the users of this book.

However there are thousands of Indian cookery books, so why do we need another one?

As you all are aware, there is always a demand for fresh, easy and workable food recipes which will encourage, enable and support people to continue cooking nutritious food. 'Healthy Indian recipes–Ultimate cooking guide' has done just that by covering all types of wholesome Indian food, by providing the essential and the beneficial food information and by offering recipe guidelines and practical cooking tips.

My goal is to share my knowledge and experience in the hope that the young and the old, the singles and the couples, the students and the working women and men, those who consider that they can't cook, those who do not bother to cook and **especially those who love Indian food will all benefit from this book**. *All recipes shared in this book are used in my own cooking which are authentic, simple, delicious, tested and proven recipes.*

The best thing about all the recipes in this book is that there is no indulgence of food that is higher in sugar, fat or salt. The recipes focus on the moderated use of these and other selective and balanced ingredients to create the delicate taste of a healthy dish.

But, who said Indian cooking is difficult?

It is simply a myth that Indian cooking is very involved and difficult to get it right. I encourage you to put these recipes to the test. Don't lose heart, appreciate your efforts and **remember that practise will make your cooking perfect.**

How to accommodate with the enormity in the food variety?

Indian food is like a vast ocean with thousands of unknown living species in it. In similar way, the variety in Indian food is enormous and it is impossible to know it all. I know the food of my region and what foods I regularly cook. Nevertheless, I have included some of the favourite Indian dishes, which are well-known all over the world.

At the same time some traditional recipes are simplified for busy lives and according to the availability of the ingredients found in our shops. *However I have set no hard and fast rules in the usage of the ingredients, but in many recipes I have offered you the choice to select your own vegetables, meat, fat, flour, fruit, nuts, the quantity of salt, chilli and sugar etc. This will surely accommodate everyone's taste and meet their dietary needs, without ruining the taste of the dish.*

What does 'Healthy Indian recipes—Ultimate cooking guide' provide?

This book offers far more than curry recipes. The entire Chapter 2 is dedicated to provide a vast selection of healthy, quick and easy starters/appetisers and snacks. The recipes selected are not only delicious but supply all the essential food categories by using meat, fish, eggs, dairy products, beans/lentils, cereal/grains, fruit and vegetables. For this reason all the starters/snacks are nutritious and healthy. They are in the form of salads (chaart), mash (bhurta), kebabs, pasties and fritters, products of cheese and yoghurt and soups.

Most of us are happy to cook the main meal but opt for pre-prepared desserts from the shops. This is a good option if you are saving time and energy but not all desserts are healthy and *there is no way to reduce the sugar and the fat content from the pre-prepared sweet dishes.* Whereas when you prepare your own, you can go for the healthier ingredients and you have the choice to reduce/eliminate the sugar and the fat contents.

All the desserts included in Chapter 7 are healthy and delicious. To help you to select the healthy ones from the big range of Indian sweet meat (mithai), effort has been made to give you the main ingredients of the each sweet meat.

Saunf chai (fennel seed tea), ginger and lemon, mint and the celery tea are very popular hot drinks in our household. This motivated me to add some refreshing cold and hot drinks which are *simple, caffeine and alcohol free, economical, quick and easy to make*—all in Chapter 8.

But that's not all; the whole of Chapter 1 is devoted to the basics of food. *The important information is provided to **refresh** your knowledge about the essential categories of food. That will enable you to select food which is balanced, healthy, nutritious, edible and wholesome.* This Chapter also highlights the importance of using the appropriate methods of cooking. It concludes with a list of the flavour and aroma infusing spices used in the Indian cuisine.

Chapter 3 is fully committed to the main meal dishes; including meat, fish, eggs, paneer, beans/lentils and the vegetable curries. All the curry recipes are selected to provide plenty of the essential foods. For this reason these curries are nutritious and healthy.

You will note in this book that dahi (yoghurt) is the most common and frequently used ingredient. For this very reason I am compelled to encourage you to learn how to make yoghurt at home by using recipe No: 24 of Chapter 2.

Paneer (cheese) is enjoyed all over the world in Indian snacks, curries and in some desserts. To make sure you have a good vegetarian cheese, make your own by following recipe No: 26 of Chapter 2.

Chapter 4 is generously handing over the preparations of nine different types of rice dishes. Under the category of the Indian bread, Chapter 5 includes the preparations of naan bread, chapati/roti, plain and stuffed parathas, baysen ki roti, poories, pooray and dosa. Baysen Ki Roti and dosa could be suitable for people with the gluten intolerance/sensitivity (please verify before using).

All the snacks, curries and rice dishes have their own specific aromas and unique tastes but the pickles and fresh chutneys lift the taste to another level. Chapter 6 provides useful information and recipes for the different types of condiments. I encourage you to make these as it will definitely add another dimension to your Indian meals

*Throughout the book there are bundles of practical and realistic cooking tips and also some interesting food information all provided under the heading, **"Note to remember".*** *This is a generous help to give you the support that is needed for your achievement in cooking good and healthy Indian food.*

If you are looking for the gluten-free diet or other special dietary needs, you will discover good news in every section of the book.

For the vegetarian there is plenty of choice in each section of the book. There are over 20 vegetarian starters, 14 vegetable main meals, 6 rice dishes and Chapters 5-8 cater for both the vegetarians and the others.

Family, friends, colleagues and all those who are lovers of Indian food, you have been provided with two great offers in this book. One is to try the great variety of quick, easy, delicious, and healthy recipes of the Indian dishes which you may not have cooked before. *Secondly you have the privilege to support the poor children of your world, by providing them with a daily meal, clothes, basic school kit and education.* Some of the profit from the sales of this book will go towards the Mary's Meal charity which I have been faithfully supporting—the children of Malawi.

In addition you can send further donations directly to the head office of the Mary's Meals. All information is provided at the back of the book.

Food for thought:
Count your blessings and reflect on them one by one as you select, prepare, cook and enjoy your food with a caring, sharing and a thankful heart.

H. Karam Ellahie

Chapter 1

Basics of Food

Food is a necessity and a common need of all mankind, and it is the distinguishing mark of each culture.

What is food?

Food is that substance which is selected, prepared and consumed to maintain life and growth.

The main function of the food is:

- ❖ To supply heat and energy to the body.
- ❖ To provide material for the formation of new body cells and to repair worn-out cells.
- ❖ To support each organ to facilitate their functions properly.
- ❖ To build up the immune system.

*It is therefore **important** to make every **effort** to have the **right food**, in the **right amount** and at the **right time**. For this reason, it is helpful to gain or to refresh the basic knowledge of the food we need to eat.*

A healthy balanced diet includes all the six essential food categories in the appropriate amounts, and they are:

1. *Carbohydrates* (starch-sugar foods)

The source: The main sources of *good starch-carbohydrates* are grains/ cereals, root vegetable, potatoes, cauliflower, all varieties of pumpkins/ squash, green peas/green beans, sweet corn and all legumes/lentils.

Whereas the *good sugar-carbohydrates* are found in most of the fruits like bananas, pineapples, pears, plums, apricots, apples, papayas, nectarine/ peaches, all the berries and mangoes etc. Unrefined cane sugar and honey are both good sugar-carbohydrates, when used moderately.

The Functions: Carbohydrates are the main fuel source for producing heat and energy to run our most fascinating and complicated body.

2. *Proteins*

The source: The foods high in proteins are all meats, fish, eggs, milk and dairy products. But there are other rich sources of protein like whole grains, legumes (lentils, peas and beans), nuts and seeds, green leafy vegetables and green vegetables.

The Functions: Proteins are essential for growth, maintenance and for the repair of all the cells in our body.

Some of the hormones, the enzymes and antibodies in our body are made of proteins. Proteins produce some heat and energy for the body too.

3. *Fats*

The source: Foods rich in fats are edible nuts, oil seeds (sunflower seeds, rapeseeds, pumpkin and melon seeds, mustard seeds and sesame seeds) avocados and fish oil. The different types of cooking oils are: canola oil, rapeseed oil, olive oil, sesame oil, peanut oil, palm oil, corn oil, grape seed oil, mustard oil, sunflower oil, animal fat (butter/ghee) and coconut oil.

The Functions: Fat is also an essential food as it doesn't only make the food tasty but produces heat and energy.

It is a good solvent for vitamin A, D, E and K (insoluble in water) which means that it is through the fat that the body absorbs these vitamins.

Fats also play an important role in promoting cell growth.

4. *Vitamins*

The source: Vitamins can be **added** to your **diet** through eating **food** like—bread, rice, fish, meat, liver, eggs, edible nuts and seeds, whole grains, dairy products, all vegetables and fruits.

The Functions: Vitamins are needed in very small quantities but are very essential to the body and any deficiency can cause disorders and disease.

One of their functions is to *promote* the normal growth of the body.

They also assist in the release of heat and energy but do not directly produce any energy or heat. So vitamins are not alternatives for protein or carbohydrate foods. They sometimes act like a catalyst to help the metabolic activities of enzymes in the body.

The other functions of vitamins are to build the immune system, to help in the formation of hormones and to convert complex fats into simple compounds.

5. *Minerals*

The source: Like vitamins, minerals can also be taken through the diet by eating fruits, vegetables, eggs, meat, liver, poultry, tofu, fish, sesame/sunflower seeds, pulses and grains. Nuts like almonds, hazel nuts and Brazil nuts, and green vegetables like broccoli, curly kale, cabbage, okra, and spinach and water cress are also a good source of minerals.

The Functions: Minerals like calcium, phosphorus, sodium, potassium, and sulphur are required in bigger quantities by our bodies in comparison with some minerals like copper, zinc and selenium which are essential but the body needs them only in traces. Minerals are used in the composition of healthy teeth and bones.

But different minerals play other important roles in the body. For example:

Iron in the blood transports the oxygen to all the tissues and the cells of our body.
Iodine regulates the metabolism.
Potassium helps to regulate the heartbeat.
Calcium makes bones and teeth stronger, and also plays an important role in regulating blood clotting, muscle toning and nerve functioning.

6. *Water*

About 70% of our body is made up of water, and about 90% of the blood is water, and these percentages need to be maintained.

The source: Plain tap water directly taken as a drink is the most vital part of our diet. Light juices, beverages, soups, juicy fruits and vegetables are the other sources of water.

The functions: The importance of the water is realised when you focus on the various functions of the water in our body.

It regulates the body's temperature.
It transports oxygen and the digested nutrients in the form of blood; to all parts of the body.
It removes waste and toxins through urine, faeces and sweat.
It is a good lubricant for all the joints and all the organs of our body.

Note to remember: Please keep in mind that I do not profess to be a nutritionist; therefore there is every possibility that food information provided; might need updating.

How to select your food:

A selection of healthy foods is vital because we need to give our body every opportunity to pick up what it needs and how much it needs. This can be done by providing a great variety in the food we eat.

The whole purpose for providing the information on essential foods is to enable you to select food with an understanding of what is nutritious, necessary and wholesome.

Food doesn't have to be expensive but it is important that **the diet you select is balanced, nutritious, fresh and at its best.** Be brave and adventurous. Try new food combinations or try different meats, grains, legumes, fruits, vegetables and good fats to make different dishes using the given recipes.

Why do we need to cook food?

We spend lots of money, effort, time and energy to prepare our food and this is the proof that food holds a prominent place in our lives. However food is cooked for the three primary reasons and they are:

1. Cooking makes the food attractive and more appetising and brings out the taste of the food. The aromas and the flavours of the added spices come out more during the cooking process. *Creating good flavours in food is in your hands, so use the correct method of cooking with appropriate spices as indicated in the recipes. It's been said by Thomas Keller "A recipe has no soul. You, as the cook, must bring soul to the recipe".*

2. Cooking softens the food; it makes the food edible, easy to chew and helps in the digestion of the food. *Therefore it is important not to rush with your cooking time but make sure that all the ingredients are well cooked.*

3. Another important function of cooking is to make food safer to eat. The high temperature used in cooking kills germs, bacteria and even parasites which come to our food from plants and animals. *It is advisable to know what foods can be eaten uncooked and what foods need to be cooked in order to avoid health hazards.*

What are the different methods of cooking?

There of thousands and thousands of recipes to choose from in order to prepare our meals but there are only three basic methods of cooking. The first one is roasting/grilling/baking, the second is boiling/stewing, and the third is frying. People have spent a great deal of their time experimenting to find for themselves that certain foods are only suitable for one or two particular methods of cooking, whereas some can go through all the cooking processes. *Therefore it is important to use the right method of cooking given in each recipe.*

What are the basic ingredients for the Indian recipes?

It is impossible to prepare a good Indian curry without onions, garlic, ginger, tomatoes, chilli, salt and fat. What makes Indian food different is the use of many spices—not only in the curries but in the preparation of different snacks, rice dishes, deserts and condiments. The spices used in Indian recipes give special aromas and enhance the taste of the food. The following spices ground or whole, are always found in the cupboards of those who love to cook Indian food.

Ground spices: chillies, coriander, cumin, garam masala, dry ginger and dry garlic, turmeric, cinnamon, fennel and black pepper.

Whole spices: cloves, cumin, fennel seeds, mustard seeds, cinnamon sticks, bay and curry leaves, black and green cardamoms (the big black cardamoms are used for savoury dishes, whereas small green cardamoms are used for sweet dishes).

Fresh coriander, mint, curry leaves and methi leaves are the popular herbs, used either for garnishing or in cooking. *Buy, wash, chop and freeze to keep them in stock.*

Besides spices & herbs it is always good to stock the kitchen cupboards with different daals, rice, chapati flour, baysen (chickpea flour sold as gram flour) and tins of red beans/chickpeas etc. These are imperishable and good foods. Perishable foods like meat, fish, fresh vegetables, and fresh ginger/garlic can be bought when required *or buy, wash, make portions needed, bag it and freeze.*

Note to remember: *Most of the whole spices like cloves, cinnamon sticks, black/white cardamoms, bay and the curry leaves are not edible; these spices are there to release fragrance and flavour to the food.* **When serving, remove them from the prepared food.**

Basic food words in Urdu:

Urdu	English	Urdu	English
Achaar	Pickle	Gaajer	Carrots
Adrick	Ginger	Goshtt	Meat
Aloo	Potato	Haldee	Turmeric
Atta	Chapati flour	Haree mirch	Green chilli
Aunda	Egg	Kali mirch	Black pepper
Aunday	Eggs	Kheer	Milk pudding
Baagun	Aubergines	Lal mirch	Red chilli
Badam	Almonds	Loong	Cloves
Bundh Gobi	Cabbage	Lasen	Garlic
Chawal	Rice	Masala	Mixture of Spices
Chana	Chickpeas	Mutter	Peas
Dahi	Yoghurt	Palak	Spinach
Dahania	Coriander	Peaaz	Onion
Daal	Lentils & Beans	Paneer	Cheese
Darchinee	Cinnamon	Sabzi	Vegetables
Eelachie	Cardamom	Zeera	Cumin

Food for thought:
Above all, the most essential ingredient in all the food recipes is to be thankful for the gift of life with family, friends and neighbours with whom we share our lives and our food.

H. Karam Ellahie

Chapter 2

Healthy Snacks and Starters

Most of the recipes are not only quick and easy to prepare but are very nutritious, substantial, convenient, and some could be a good alternative to bread or a sandwich. You will be amazed that about thirty different types of snacks recipes are provided by using a great range of food. That includes meat, fish, eggs, dairy products, legumes, cereal/grains, fruit, vegetable and spices. Except pakoras, namick paray and samosas which are deep fried, all other snacks/starters use small amounts of the fat in the preparation.

The best thing about all the recipes in this book is that there is no indulgence of food that is higher in sugar, fat or salt. The recipes focus on the moderated use of these and other selective and balanced ingredients to create the delicate taste of a healthy dish.

Note to remember: *Please go through the recipes cautiously to check if you are sensitive or intolerant to any of the ingredients and make sure to eliminate or to use a suitable alternative.*

Healthy Snacks, Appetisers and Starters:

1.   Dahi chana chaart (Plain yoghurt and chickpea salad)

Note to remember: All chickpea salads are nutritious, fat and gluten-free snack.

Serves 1-2

Ingredients:
Tin of chickpeas
Plain yoghurt
Salt to taste, pinch of chilli powder or black pepper
Fresh small chilli (optional)
½ teaspoon of tamarind paste (see recipe No: 10 of Chapter.6) optional

Method:
Open the tin of chickpeas and pour into a colander/sieve and wash under running tap water. Put the washed chickpeas in the bowl and add 4-5 tablespoons of plain yoghurt, or if preferred add some cottage cheese or homemade paneer or tamarind paste. Add salt and chilli or paprika powder or black pepper to your taste and mix all the ingredients and enjoy.

Serving suggestions:
Serve as it is or with some salad greens or water cress. Addition of a baked potato goes very well in this chaart too.

2.   Chana aloo chaart (Chickpea potato salad)

Serves 1-2

Ingredients:
Tin of chickpeas
2-4 medium potato baked, peeled and roughly broken into small chunks
1 medium fresh tomato
1 small onion
1 teaspoon of lemon juice
1-2 tablespoons of tamarind water or ½ teaspoon of tamarind paste (diluted tamarind paste with water, see recipe No: 10 of Chapter.6)

Fresh coriander or water cress or chives
Fresh small chilli (optional)
Salt to taste
Pinch of chilli powder or black pepper

Method:
Open the tin of chickpeas and pour into a colander/sieve and wash under running tap water. Put the washed chickpeas in the bowl; add the baked potato, chopped tomato and onion. Then add a dessert spoonful of chopped coriander/water cress or chives, salt and chilli (fresh chilly) or paprika powder or black pepper to your taste. Add the lemon juice and the tamarind. Give a good mix with a spoon.

Serving suggestions:
Enjoy it as it is.

3.   Tazza pahl chana chaart (fresh fruit and chickpea salad)

Serves 1-2

Ingredients:
Tin of chickpeas

A banana, an apple, kiwi, ¼ of a mango, 4-5 grapes and few segments of an orange or any other fruits of your choice
1 tablespoon lemon/orange juice
2 tablespoon of tamarind water (diluted tamarind paste with water, see recipe No: 10 of Chapter.6)
2 teaspoon of unrefined sugar
Salt (black salt if available) chilli powder or black pepper to taste

Method:
Open the tin of chickpeas and pour into a colander/sieve and wash under running tap water. Put the washed chickpeas in the bowl. Add different chopped fruits (bite size) of your choice. Add sugar and about two pinches of black salt or table salt, a small pinch of black pepper/ chilli powder. Finally add lemon juice and tamarind water and give a good mix with the spoon. Another fat and gluten-free snack is ready to be enjoyed.

Serving suggestions:
This is a healthy starter and a good appetiser. Good on its own.

4.   Chickpeas and potato stir-fry

Serves 1-2

Ingredients:
Tin of chickpeas
1 large potato baked in the microwave or in the oven or boiled
Homemade paneer/cottage cheese (optional)
1 tablespoon of tomato puree
1 teaspoon of cumin seeds
¼ teaspoon of turmeric
1 tablespoon of washed Anardana (dried seeds of pomegranate washed and soaked in hot water
½ teaspoonful of ground garam masala
½ teaspoon of fresh grated or powdered ginger
1 clove of garlic (crushed)
¼ teaspoon chilli powder
Some fresh coriander to garnish
2 tablespoons of cooking oil of your choice

Method:
Open the tin of chickpeas and pour into a colander or a sieve and wash under running tap water and keep it to one side.

Bake or boil the potato and break into chunks of reasonable size. Heat the oil in the frying pan and roast the cumin seeds, then add all the other spices, chillies to your taste, tomato puree and stir for 2-3 seconds. Put in the potatoes, the chickpeas and also add the paneer to absorb all the flavours. Mix everything and keep on the medium heat for 3-4 minutes. Garnish with the fresh coriander or chives or water cress.

Serving suggestions:
Serve with some crusty bread or with any of the Indian breads from Chapter. 5 or it can be eaten on its own or with some salad.

Note of suggestion:
Chickpeas are not only good for snacks/starters but in making curry and rice dishes with/without meat and vegetables. Use the basic curry sauce, and almost all the meats and the vegetables work well with the chickpeas.

5.　Dahi aloo bhurta (Plain yoghurt and baked potato salad)

Note to remember: All bhurta (mash) are nutritious, fat and gluten-free snack

Serves 1-2

Ingredients:
1-2 large potato baked in the microwave or in the oven or boiled
2 spring onions
Fresh leaves of mint or fresh coriander (1 tablespoon)
200-250g of plain yoghurt
Chopped tomato
Ground cumin
Green chopped chilli (optional) or black pepper to taste
½ to 1 teaspoon of tamarind paste (see recipe No: 10 of Chapter.6) optional

Method:
Take plain yoghurt in a bowl. Add salt to your taste, half teaspoon of ground cumin, red or green chillies or black pepper to your taste. Add finely chopped mint, spring onion and tomato. Break the peeled baked potato into small chunks and then mix everything together.

Serving suggestions:
A healthy starter but this can also be used as a raita for the curry or rice dishes. Instead of yoghurt, the addition of homemade paneer or cottage cheese also goes very well with this snack/starter.

6. Aloo bhurta (Baked potato mash)

Serves 1-2

Ingredients:
2-4 medium/large potatoes baked in the microwave or in the oven or boiled
1 medium fresh tomato
1 small onion
Ground cumin
Green chilli (optional) or black pepper
Fresh leaves of mint or fresh coriander (½ tablespoon) or some water cress or chives
½ teaspoon of lemon juice or a teaspoon of tamarind paste
A knob of butter

Method:
Mash the baked potatoes roughly in a bowl and add the chopped tomato, onion, ½ teaspoon of ground cumin, salt, red or green chillies or black pepper to your taste. Add fresh mint or coriander and mix everything with a knob of butter and ½ teaspoon of lemon juice or a teaspoon of tamarind paste or add both.

Serving suggestions:
It can be eaten on its own, or could be good sandwich filler or a filling for stuffed parathas.

7. Baagun dahi bhurta (Baked Aubergines and plain yoghurt salad)

Serves 1-2

Ingredients:
1 large aubergine baked in the microwave or in the oven
1 tablespoon of fresh chopped leaves of mint or fresh coriander
200-250g of plain yoghurt
1 chopped tomato
1 small chopped onion
Ground cumin, green chilli (optional), black pepper

½ teaspoon of tamarind paste (see recipe No: 10 of Chapter.6) optional
½ teaspoon lemon juice

Method:
Take plain yoghurt in a bowl and add the chopped tomatoes, onions, ½ teaspoon of ground cumin, salt, red or green chillies or black pepper to your taste. Add finely chopped coriander or fresh mint. Break the peeled baked aubergine into small chunks and then mix everything together. This is a very healthy, delicious and easy way to eat aubergines.

Serving suggestions:
This can be used as a raita for the rice dishes or can be eaten as is, or as an additional dish. Instead of yoghurt the addition of homemade paneer or cottage cheese also goes very well with this snack/starter.

8. Shimla mirch and Baagun bhurta with dahi (Baked red/green pepper, baked aubergines mash with plain yoghurt)

Serves 1-2

Ingredients:
1 baked aubergine
1 red or green pepper cooked in the microwave or in the oven
1 medium fresh tomato and 1 small onion
Ground cumin, ½ green chilli (optional), black pepper
1 teaspoon of tamarind paste
200-250g plain yoghurt

Method:
In a suitable bowl; mash or roughly break the baked aubergine and red/green pepper into very small chunks and add the chopped tomato, onion, ¼ teaspoon of ground cumin, salt, green chilli or black pepper to your taste. Add fresh mint or coriander and mix everything with plain yoghurt and a teaspoon of tamarind paste. This is a very healthy, delicious and easy way to eat aubergines and peppers.

Serving suggestions: This can be used as a raita for the rice dishes or eaten as is, or as an additional dish. Instead of yoghurt the addition of homemade paneer or cottage cheese also works very well with this snack/starter.

9. Aloo, Shimla mirch and Baagun bhurta (Baked potato, baked red/green pepper and baked aubergines mash with tomatoes and onions)

Serves 1-2

Ingredients:
2-3 medium potatoes baked in the microwave or in the oven
1 red/green pepper baked in the microwave or in the oven
1 small aubergine baked in the microwave or in the oven
1 medium fresh tomato and 1 small onion
Ground cumin, ½ green chilli (optional), black pepper
Fresh leaves of mint or fresh coriander
½ teaspoon of lemon juice or ½ teaspoon of tamarind paste
A knob of butter

Method:
In a suitable bowl; mash or roughly break the baked potatoes, aubergine and red/green pepper into very small chunks and add the chopped tomato, onion, ¼ teaspoon of ground cumin, salt, green chilli or black pepper to your taste. Add fresh chopped mint or coriander and mix everything with a knob of butter and ½ teaspoon of lemon juice or half teaspoon of tamarind paste. This is a very healthy, delicious and easy way to eat the red/green peppers and the aubergines.

Serving suggestions: It can be eaten as it is or as an additional dish. The addition of yoghurt, homemade paneer or cottage cheese also goes very well with this starter. It can be good sandwich filler, too.

10. Shakarkandi bhurta (Baked sweet potato mash)

Sweet potato is a humble vegetable but full of nutrition. It could be orange, yellow or white-fleshed. It is a good source of vitamin A, C, E and B6, provides many essential minerals, high in dietary fibres. The dark orange colour of the sweet potato is high in beta carotene. Baking is the best and the easiest way to have this healthy snack.

Serves 1-2

Ingredients:
2-3 medium baked sweet potatoes in the microwave or in the oven
1 teaspoon of lemon juice
Black pepper and salt
Butter
Salt

Method:
Put the mashed baked sweet potato into a bowl and add the other ingredients. Mix it with the fork and it is ready to be consumed. If you prefer the sweet version of the above; then to the roughly mashed sweet potato sprinkle unrefined sugar and ground cinnamon. Add a knob of butter and mix it with the fork and enjoy.

11. Aloo tikkis (Potato cakes): This is a vegetarian version of the cutlets and is also known as potato cutlets.

Serves 2-3

Ingredients:
6-8 medium potatoes baked in the microwave or in the oven or boiled on the hob
1 medium onion
½ finely chopped fresh green/red pepper
Fresh leaves of mint or fresh coriander or dried/ fresh methi leaves
Salt to your taste
1 teaspoon of cumin seeds
1 teaspoon of ground garam masala
Red or green chillies or black pepper to your taste
1 egg for coating the tikkis
Sunflower or vegetable oil for frying

Method:
Take a suitable bowl and put in the peeled baked or cooked potatoes. Make a rough mash and add finely chopped onion and the pepper, all the spices and the salt to your taste. Thoroughly mix all the ingredients.

To avoid the mash sticking to your hands, just rub some oil or water into your hands. Take a reasonable amount of the mixture and roll it between your hands and the gently flattened into circular cakes.

For coating the potato cakes I like to use the whole egg slightly whisked, but some prefer to use only the white of an egg—both will give good results.

Place the frying pan on the hob and add just enough oil (not excess) to fry the cakes (avoid deep frying). Dip each potato cake first into the whisked egg and then carefully place it in the hot frying pan with oil. On medium heat, cook both sides until golden-brown. Take them out and place them on a paper towel to get rid of the excess oil.

Note to remember: If you prefer, you can make a thin seasoned batter with chickpea flour and cold water, for coating all types of tikkis and kebabs.

Serving suggestions:
The potato cakes are good healthy snack, which can be eaten with all tomato sauces or any relish of your choice or any chutney from Chapter 6. These can be good sandwich fillers, and also consider making tortilla, chapati, paratha, pancake, or dosa wraps with some salad leaves or salsa.

12. Aloo, palak and cheese tikkis (Spinach and cheese potato cakes)

Follow recipe 11 for the Aloo tikkis (potato cakes) with an addition of extra ingredients of (handful) finely chopped spinach and a tablespoon of grated cheese. (Any hard cheese will do for the flavouring).

13. Aloo tikkis with tuna fish (Fish cakes)

Serves 3-4

Ingredients:
1 tin of tuna fish
6-8 medium potatoes baked in the microwave or in the oven or boiled
1 medium onion
½ finely chopped green/red pepper

Fresh leaves of mint or fresh coriander or dried/ fresh methi leaves
Salt to your taste
1 teaspoon of cumin seeds
1½ teaspoons of ground garam masala
Red or green chillies and black pepper to your taste
1-2 whisked eggs
Sunflower or vegetable oil, for frying the cakes

Method:
Take a suitable bowl for the peeled baked or cooked potatoes. Make a rough mash and add finely chopped onion and the pepper, all the spices and salt to your taste. Before adding tuna fish, make sure that it is well drained. It is best to use your hands to squeeze out all the brine. Thoroughly mix all the ingredients.

To avoid the mixture sticking to your hands, just rub some oil or water before rolling the mixture into your hands. Take a reasonable amount of the mixture and roll it between your hands and gently flatten into circular cakes.

For coating the potato cakes I like to use the whole egg slightly whisked, but some prefer to use only the white of an egg—both will give good results.

Place the frying pan on the hob and add just enough oil (not excess) to fry the cakes (avoid deep frying). Dip each potato cake first into the whisked egg and then carefully place it in the hot frying pan with oil. On medium heat, cook both sides until golden-brown. Take them out and place them on a paper towel to get rid of the excess oil.

Serving suggestions:
The tuna fish and potato cakes are a good healthy snack (high in protein and good starch carbohydrate). These can be eaten with all tomato sauces or any relish of your choice or any chutney from Chapter 6. These can be good sandwich fillers, and also consider making tortilla, chapati, paratha, pancake, or Dosa wraps with some salad leaves or salsa.

14. Shami kebabs (mince/ground meat and chana daal kebab)

Serves 4-6

Ingredients:
300g of lamb or beef mince
100g chana daal—washed and soaked in water for 2-3 hours
2 medium onions
1 tablespoon of garam masala
2 teaspoons of cumin seeds
¼ teaspoon of turmeric
1 teaspoon of red chillies
1 teaspoon of ground ginger or 1 tablespoon fresh grated ginger
Fresh coriander (handful)
1-2 small chopped green chilli
2 eggs for coating the kebabs
Sunflower or vegetable oil for frying the kebabs

Method:
In a suitable cooking pan, put all the ingredients leaving fresh coriander, green chilli and eggs. Add about a cup of water and mix all the ingredients with the wooden spoon. On medium heat cook the meat mixture until the meat and the daal is cooked and all liquid is totally dried. While the meat mixture is cooling down, chop the washed fresh coriander and at least 1-2 green chilli to go in the meat mixture, and whisk two eggs for coating the kebabs

When the meat is ready to be handled, pass the cooked meat mixture with the chopped coriander and the chopped green chilli through a food processor to make a homogeneous mixture. Take out the mixture and shape it into reasonably sized cakes by pressing, rolling and patting the mixture between your hands and gently flatten into circular cakes. Place the frying pan on the hob and add just enough oil (not excess) to fry the cakes (avoid deep frying). Dip each kebab first into the whisked egg and then carefully place it in the hot frying pan with oil. On medium heat, cook both sides until golden-brown. Take them out and place onto a paper towel to get rid of the excess oil.

Serving suggestions:
This is a high protein—good carbohydrate snack, which can be eaten with all tomato sauces, mint or coriander chutney or any relish of your choice. Like the potato cake, shami-kebabs can also be good sandwich filler, and also consider making tortilla, chapati, paratha, pancake, or Dosa wraps with some salad leaves or salsa.

15. Meatball/Koffata kebabs or kebab on skewers

Serves 4-6

Ingredients:
300-400g of lamb or beef or turkey or chicken mincemeat
1 medium size chopped onion
1 teaspoon of garam masala
1 tablespoon of ground coriander
1 teaspoon of cumin seeds
¼ teaspoon of turmeric
½ teaspoon of red chillies
1 tablespoon of desiccated coconut
1 teaspoon of crushed poppy seeds or ground almonds
Handful of fresh coriander
Handful of fresh spinach
2 small green chillies
Fresh chopped ginger, about 1 teaspoon
1 egg for binding the meat
Cooking oil for shallow frying

Method:
Pass all the ingredients including the meat through a food processor to make a homogeneous mixture. Take the mixture out and roll it into small balls or shape them like beef burgers (The latter will cook evenly). Into the frying pan add enough oil and put it on medium heat. Carefully place the Koffatas in the hot oil and on medium heat cook until brown. But make sure that all the Koffatas are cooked thoroughly by turning them over several times. Take them out and place them onto a paper towel to get rid of the excess fat.

Alternative methods of shaping and cooking the kebabs:

Put the mixture on skewers, about 4 inches long and ½ inch in thickness. Put the kebab skewers under the grill or on the barbecue fire and keep turning the skewers until the kebabs are cooked.

Serving suggestions:
This is a high protein snack, which can be eaten as they are or with any tomato sauce, mint or coriander chutney in yoghurt or any relish of your choice. These can also be good sandwich fillers, and also consider making tortilla, chapati, paratha, pancake, or Dosa wraps with some salad leaves or salsa. Cooked with the curry sauce it is one of the main meal dishes—see recipe No: 12 of Chapter 3B.

16. Nargisi koffata kebab (Meat and boiled egg kebabs)

These kebabs are like scotch eggs but made with lamb or beef meat and well-seasoned with the Indian herbs and spices. Without the curry sauce both meatballs and the Nargisi koffatas are served as a snack. Please follow the recipe No: 19 of Chapter 3B for making the nargisi koffatas.

Serving suggestions:
This is a high protein snack, which can be eaten as they are or with any tomato sauce, mint or coriander chutney in yoghurt or any relish of your choice. These can also be good sandwich fillers with some lettuce/salad greens. With the curry sauce it's one of the main meal dishes—see recipe19 of Ch.3B.

17. Chicken tikka masala

Serves 2-3

Ingredients:
2-3 chicken breasts
3 tablespoons of plain yoghurt
1 teaspoon of paprika
½ teaspoon of chilli powder
1 teaspoon of garam masala
1 teaspoon of ground coriander

1 teaspoon of ground fresh or ginger powder, 1-2 cloves of garlic and 1 medium onion (blend the three ingredients into a paste, using the food processor)
Fresh coriander for the garnish
Salt to taste
2-3 tablespoons of cooking oil

Method:
Cut the chicken breast into reasonably sized pieces.

Put all the ingredients in a bowl and mix everything together. Then add the chicken and stir it so that all the chicken is coated with the yoghurt mixture. Leave it in the fridge for at least 2-3 hours.

There are three alternative ways to cook the chicken tikka masala. Choose the one that is convenient for you.

1. In a frying pan place 2-3 tablespoons of cooking oil and put it on high heat. Put the marinated pieces of chicken in the hot oil. Keep stirring all the time and fry until the chicken is properly cooked. Take the chicken out in the serving dish and garnish with fresh coriander.
2. Put the marinated pieces of chicken on skewers on a wire rack. Cook for 7-8 minutes under the grill/oven (on high heat). Check if the chicken is cooked by piercing the chicken with a fork, if the juices run clear it's cooked.
3. Line the oven tray with some oil and place the marinated pieces of chicken in the tray. Put the tray in the preheated oven at 180°C/355°F/Gas mark 4 and cook it for 10-15 minutes. Change the side of the chicken pieces once.

Serving suggestions:
It is a good starter, either to be eaten on its own or with chutneys or pickles. It is a good accompaniment to vegetable pasta, couscous, vegetables, rice or noodles. It is also a good additional dish with lentils and vegetable curries. Consider with salad greens or with salsa for making tortilla/chapati/paratha wraps.

18. Tandoori Chicken

Serves 3-4

Ingredients:
6-8 skinned chicken drum sticks or chicken thighs
3-4 tablespoons of plain yoghurt
2 teaspoons of paprika
½ teaspoon of chilli powder
1 teaspoon of garam masala
2 teaspoons of ground coriander
1 teaspoon of ground fresh or ginger powder
1 tablespoon of lemon juice
Salt to taste

Method:
Wash the chicken pieces and drain all the water and then put them in a suitable bowl. Mix the yoghurt with all the other ingredients and pour over the chicken. Stir so that all the chicken is coated with the yoghurt mixture. To get good results, leave it in the fridge overnight or at least for 4-5 hours. Line the oven tray with plenty of cooking oil before putting the chicken on it and cover the chicken with foil. Place the oven tray in the middle of the preheated oven at 180°C/355°F/Gas mark 4 and cook for 30-40 minutes. Remove foil, turn over each piece and continue to cook until the chicken is thoroughly done. Take the tandoori chicken out from the oven and keep it warm by covering it with kitchen foil.

Serving suggestions: Tandoori chicken is a good starter, either to be eaten on its own or with the yoghurt chutneys or with pickles. It is a good accompaniment to vegetable pasta or couscous or vegetable rice or noodles. It is also a good additional dish with lentils and vegetable curries. The meat from the tandoori chicken with salad greens or salsa is suitable for making chapati or paratha or tortilla wraps.

19. Pakoras

Serves 4-6

Like samosas, the pakoras are very popular and a favourite Indian fast-food—sold in the shops or made at home as a snack/appetiser. The two main ingredients are the baysen sometimes known as the gram flour (chickpea flour) for making the batter and the chopped vegetables which go into the batter. The batter mixture is then deep fried.

Ingredients:
250-300g of chickpea flour (baysen)
1 teaspoon of garam masala
1 tablespoon of ground coriander
1 tablespoon of cumin seed
1 tablespoon of sesame seeds
¾-1 teaspoon of red chilli powder
Baking powder ¼-½ of a teaspoon
1 tablespoon of grated fresh ginger
1 small chopped green chilli
2 large onions (chopped)
4-5 medium potatoes (chopped)
Handful of chopped fresh spinach
Handful of methi and coriander leaves
Cauliflower chopped (handful)
Aubergine chopped (handful)
1 tablespoon of washed anardana (dried seeds of pomegranate) is optional
Salt to taste
Cooking oil for the deep or shallow frying

Method:
Put chickpea flour (baysen) with all the dry ingredients into a suitably sized bowl and mix it well. To the dry mixture add little amount of cold water; mix it well and keep on adding splashes of cold water to make a fairly thick batter. Add all the chopped ingredients and a tablespoon of oil to the batter and mix it well with a spoon. Leave it to rest. The final consistency of the batter needs to be slightly thicker than pancake batter. If you need to thicken it, then add little bit more of the dry baysen. If you want to make it thinner, just add little more cold water.

Note to remember:

❖ The right temperature of oil can be tested by dropping a tiny amount of the batter in the hot oil. If the batter rises immediately to the top without turning brown, the oil is ready and it is at the correct temperature to start frying the pakoras.

❖ But if the batter immediately turns brown, it means that the oil is too hot and you need to turn the heat down.

❖ If the batter sinks down, this is the sign that the oil is not hot enough. So turn the heat up.

❖ Maintain the right temperature of oil by reheating the oil after frying every batch and before starting the next one.

❖ Make sure that pakoras are well cooked from inside, test by cutting one of the pakoras into half to check that the middle is not doughy, but cooked.

❖ Fry pakoras in several small batches in order to maintain the temperature of the hot oil steady in order to cook all pakoras evenly and properly.

Frying the Pakoras:

Note to remember: *»Use round & deep spatula with holes—it makes easy to drain the hot fat. Use this spatula for all deep/shallow frying food; e.g. for pakoras, samosas, kebabs and poories etc . . . .*

Using a suitably deep frying pan or deep fryer, fill one third with the cooking oil and put it on a medium heat. Carefully take a tablespoonful of the mixture and gently and carefully drop into the hot oil. Keep on spooning out the mixture into the hot fryer until it can hold no more. Cook for about 4-5 minutes but keep turning the sides of the pakoras with a suitable »spatula; until they are crispy, golden-brown and cooked. Take them out of the hot oil and drain on the kitchen towels. Continue to fry the rest of the mixture into reasonable batches. Pakoras are delicious and healthy because they are made with a healthy batter and with several vegetables.

Serving suggestions:
Pakoras can be eaten as they are, or with plain yoghurt as a dip. All pickles, chutneys, and all tomato sauces can go very well with the pakoras. They

can be used to make a main meal dish in a sauce that is made with the baysen and yoghurt—see recipe No: 13 of Chapter 3C.

20. Pakoras batter for the onion rings, aubergine slices, spinach leaves, potato slices and for frying whole fresh chillies.

Serves 3-4

Ingredients:
2 cups of chickpea flour (baysen)
1 teaspoon of garam masala
1 tablespoon of ground coriander
1 teaspoon of red chilli powder
Pinch of baking powder
1 teaspoon of ginger powder or ½ tablespoon fresh grated ginger
Salt to taste
Cooking oil for the frying

Method:
Put all the dry ingredients into a bowl and blend with a spoon. Using cold water, make the batter and keep the same consistency as of the pancake batter. Leave it to rest.

If you have decided on onion rings then cut the onions into thin rings.

If you have chosen aubergines, then cut it into thin round slices.

If you are a spinach lover then spinach pakoras is a tasty way to eat spinach, so just wash the spinach leaves.

Potato is a common choice, just cut the potatoes into thin slices.

If you are a chilli lover, wash the whole medium hot fresh chillies.

Using a suitable frying pan, fill one third with the cooking oil and put it on a medium heat. Dip the slices of the vegetable of your choice or the leaves of the spinach into the batter so that the vegetables are completely covered with the batter. Then place straight in the hot oil. When one side is cooked, turn it over to cook the other side. Take it out of the hot oil and drain on a paper towel. Pakoras are delicious and healthy because they are made with a healthy batter and with several vegetables.

Serving suggestions:
These can be eaten as they are, or use plain yoghurt or yoghurt with the green chutneys as a dip. All pickles, chutneys, and tomato sauces can go very well with the pakoras. Pakoras are delicious, substantial and a good healthy snack/starter.

21. Samosas

Serves 3-4

Like pakoras, the samosas are very popular and a favourite Indian fast-food—sold in the shops or made at home as a snack /appetiser. These are made with a thin pastry which is filled with dry vegetable or meat curry. The size of the samosa may vary a lot but the shape is always triangular. The pastry of the samosa is made crispy and tasty by deep frying.

Ingredients:
Prepare the filling first so that it reaches room temperature by the time you have prepared the pastry and rolled it.

Method:

Mixed vegetable filling:

Make a dry curry of potato, carrot and peas by frying some chopped onion and adding very small cubes of 4 medium potatoes and a carrot and a cup of peas. Keep stirring, while you add spices of your choice or follow recipe No: 1of Ch.3C for the vegetable curry. Add just enough water to cook the vegetables, but make sure that the liquid is all dried on the hob. Take the pan off the hob and let it cool. Then add chopped fresh coriander and mix it with the cooked vegetables.

Potato filling:

This is a favourite and easy samosa filling—see recipe No: 6 of Ch.2. Aloo bhurta (Baked or boiled potato mash with tomato and onion).

Potato curry:

Another way to make a delicious potato filling is to prepare a dry potato curry.

Ingredients:
4-5 medium peeled potatoes cut in small cubes
1 chopped large onion
1 fresh tomato or 1 tablespoon of tomato puree
¼ teaspoon of garlic
½ teaspoon of ginger
¼ teaspoon of turmeric
½ teaspoon of red chilli powder or 1 teaspoon of paprika
1 teaspoon of garam masala
1 teaspoon of cumin seeds
1 tablespoon of anardana (washed and soaked in hot water)
Salt to taste
2-3 tablespoons of cooking oil of your choice
Handful of chopped methi or fresh coriander

Method:
Heat the cooking oil in a pan and fry the chopped onions until golden-brown. Add the spices, ginger, garlic, anardana and the tomato. Stir for 10-20 seconds and then add the potato cubes. Stir to mix everything and add ¼ cup of water to cook the potatoes. Take the pan off the hob when the potatoes are cooked and all the liquid has dried. Let it cool; then add the chopped fresh coriander/methi and mix with the potato curry.

Meat filling:

Method:
Make a dry curry of mincemeat (beef or lamb or chicken or turkey) with some peas or potatoes (optional) by frying chopped onion. Add 200g of mincemeat and keep stirring while you add the ginger, garam masala,

ground cumin, red chilli (or follow recipe No: 14 of Chapter 3B for mincemeat and the potato/peas curry). Add just enough water to cook the meat and the peas, but make sure that the liquid is all dried on the hob. Take it off the heat and let it cool. Then add chopped fresh coriander and mix it with the cooked mincemeat and the peas.

Pastry preparation:

Rolled samosa sheets are available from all Indian food stores. But you can make your own:

Ingredients:
250-300g of plain flour
1-2 tablespoons of any cooking oil to go into the pastry preparation
Pinch of salt
¼ teaspoon of baking powder
Cold milk/cold water to make the dough

Method:
The easy way to make the samosa pastry is to use a dough maker. Put flour, salt, baking powder and cooking oil in the dough maker and mix until the oil mixes thoroughly with the flour. Then add splashes of milk until a smooth and firm ball is formed. Take the dough out and knead with your hands for 2-3 minutes. Cover it with the cling film and leave the pastry in the fridge at least for 30 minutes.

How to make and to fry the samosas:

Take out the pastry and divide it in small equal portions. Take one portion and roll it into a ball between your palms. On the kitchen work surface roll each portion very thin using a rolling pin. (See recipe No: 1 of Chapter 5 for rolling the chapatis). By using a knife, cut the circular pastry into two halves. In the centre of each half, spoon out the vegetable or the meat filling.

*A **good tip*** for sealing the edges of the pastry is to make a thin sealing paste with plain flour and water. Apply this thin paste on the edges of the rolled and cut pastry, fold the pastry over the filling and press it with your fingers to seal the edges (making triangular shaped samosas). Make sure the samosas are sealed properly, otherwise while deep frying there is always a possibility that the filling could come out of the samosa pastry.

It is good to prepare all the samosas and then fry them in batches. Carefully deep fry on medium heat until the pastry is crispy, golden-brown and cooked.

Note to remember: Though samosas are deep fried they are still healthy because the filling is made of vegetables/meat, good herbs and spices. The filling is made with fresh meat/vegetable which has no processed or artificial ingredients. There is nothing healthier than the low fat plain yoghurt dip or fresh green chutneys.

Serving suggestions:
Samosa can be eaten as it is, or you can use low fat plain yoghurt or the yoghurt and the green chutney dip. All pickles, fresh green chutneys, any tomato sauce can go very well with the samosa. Samosas are delicious and a substantial snack or a good starter.

22. Namick Paray (Savoury nibbles)

Namick Paray are the crispy fried strips made with the savoury wheat flour or with the chickpea/rice flour.

Serves: 1-2

Ingredients:
1 cup of white flour (if preferred chickpea flour)
1 tablespoon of semolina/rice flour
¼ teaspoon of crushed cumin seeds
1 tablespoon of sesame seeds
2-3 crushed peppercorns or pinch of red chilli powder is optional
Pinch of baking soda/powder
¼ teaspoon of salt
Cold water or milk to make the dough
Cooking oil for frying

Method:
The easy way to make namick paray pastry is to a dough maker. Put flour, semolina, salt, baking soda and a tablespoon of oil into the dough maker and mix all ingredients until oil and the other ingredients are mixed thoroughly with the flour. Then add splashes of milk or water until a smooth and firm ball is formed. Aim not to make the dough too soft. Take the pastry out and knead with your hands for 2-3 minute. Cover it with cling-film and leave the pastry in the fridge for at least 30 minutes. Take the pastry out from the fridge and divide it in 2-3 equal portions. Roll each portion into ¼ inch thick rectangular sheets by using the rolling pin. Cut into rectangular shape or diamond shaped strips about 2-3 inches long. Shallow or deep fry the cut strips on medium heat, until golden-brown. Take them out and drain on paper towels.

Note to remember: Namick paray is a healthy snack/starter because it is free from processed ingredients, free from added colourings and free from flavour enhancers.

Serving suggestions:
Namick paray can be eaten as they are, or you can use plain yoghurt or yoghurt chutney as a dip. All pickles, chutneys, and any tomato sauce can go very well with the namick paray. It is a good snack or starter or can be used as nibbles.

23. Masala fish and fish with wholesome batter

Serves 3-4

A. Masala Fish

Ingredients:
4-6 pieces of any fish of your choice (wash and drain it)
Make the masala paste by mixing:
1 teaspoon of garlic puree
1 tablespoon of onion puree
½ teaspoon fresh gingers puree or 1 teaspoon of ground ginger
¼ teaspoon of ground black pepper
¼ teaspoon of chilli powder
1 teaspoon of ground cumin

1 teaspoon of coriander powder
1 tablespoon of lemon juice,
Salt to taste

Method:
Blend all the ingredients with a spoon and coat the fish pieces with the masala paste. Marinate the fish for at least for 30-40 minutes. Shallow fry the marinated fish in butter or cooking oil and cook it for 1-3 minutes on each side. (**Note** *that the cooking time depends on how thick are the fish pieces).*Take the fried fish out from the pan and drain on a paper towel to get rid of the excess oil.

Note to remember: This is not only delicious and a filling snack/starter but a good source of protein and some of the omega3 oils.

Serving suggestions:
Masala fish can be eaten on its own or can be an additional dish with the lentil and vegetable curries. All pickles or chutneys, or any tomato sauce can go well with the fish. Traditionally the fish, pakoras and naan bread are eaten together, with any green chutney.

B.   Fish with wholesome batter

Serves 3-4

Ingredients:
1 cup of chickpea flour (baysen)
½ teaspoon of garam masala
1 teaspoon of ground coriander
½ teaspoon of red chilli powder
Pinch of baking powder
½ teaspoon of cumin seeds/powder
Salt to taste
Cooking oil for shallow or deep frying

Method:
Take 4-6 pieces of any fish of your choice, wash and drain it. Sprinkle some salt, black pepper and splash little lemon over the fish and leave it aside while you make the batter. Make the batter with cold water, using

all the above ingredients, keeping the same consistency as of the pancake batter. Dip each piece of the fish in the batter and shallow/deep fry in the hot oil until golden-brown. Take the fried fish out from the hot oil and drain it on paper towels.

Serving suggestions: Fish with batter can be eaten as is or with pakoras or potato chips. All pickles, chutneys, and any tomato sauce can go very well with the fish. This is not only delicious but a substantial and a high protein snack/starter and also supplies some of omega3 oil, too. Fried fish can be an additional dish with the lentils, vegetable curries and rice.

24. Plain yoghurt as a snack and how to make yoghurt

Plain yoghurt and its importance:

Yoghurt is milk fermented naturally or by the active culture of friendly bacteria.

Plain yoghurt (dahi), by most of the Indians is known as a life giving food. It could be true because of the nutritional goodness found in the yoghurt.

Plain yoghurt is not only a good source of calcium but it provides a balanced source of easily digestible proteins, carbohydrates, fat, vitamins and minerals. The culture used in fermenting the milk, makes both calcium and B vitamins more easily absorbed and the precipitated protein is easy to digest. For this reason dahi (yoghurt) is especially used as a healing food, a gentle and an appropriate food for the upset stomach. It is considered as a cure and preventative food for diarrhoea. The reason **could be** that yoghurt builds up the friendly bacteria in the gut.

For many years, regular meal of the Indo/Pakistan farmers had been a chapati or paratha with plain or sweet yoghurt for breakfast or for lunch. The plain yoghurt and the raitas, condiments and chutneys of all sorts, and yoghurt dips have always been an additional part of the Indian food, too. Plain yoghurt is also an important cooking ingredient in many recipes provided in this book. So if this food is so good, versatile and is consumed as a proper food, there is no reason why it shouldn't be used as a snack or as a breakfast or even as a dessert. For breakfast cereal milk can be substituted by yoghurt.

Dahi (yoghurt) is the most common and the frequently used ingredient in many recipes in my book. For this very reason I am compelled to encourage you to start making this food product at home.

Homemade yoghurt is not only good in taste but it is also economical and without preservatives. It will be a green product because there is no wastage on packaging and no disposal of the packaging means reduction in environmental pollution.

How to make dahi (curd-yoghurt) at home:

500ml of whole or semi skimmed milk

4 tablespoons live active Greek yoghurt or 3 tablespoons natural live set yoghurt from the Indian food stores. I have had good results from both the starters.

Pour the measured milk into a casserole dish and heat it in the microwave at high setting for 3 minutes, stir the milk and heat it for another 2 minutes. Leave it to cool. Or alternatively, boil the milk in the pan and pour it into a casserole dish and leave it to cool.

It is important to check if the hot milk has reached to right temperature to add the starter yoghurt. Use your finger to test if it is cooled down from too hot to fairly hot or use the food thermometer and if it has cooled down to 100^0–110^0F/40-43^{0}C. Then take out 7-8 tablespoons of the warm milk and mix it with the starter yoghurt. Pour this starter into the warm milk and stir side to side and up and down, so that the culture is evenly spread. Put the lid back and insulate the dish with a thick warm tea towel or a warm towel and leave the dish in a warm part of your kitchen. The ideal place which gives good results to so many people is a warm oven. It is best to leave it overnight but it should be ready within 7-8 hours. When the yoghurt is set, you should then refrigerate it

Some of the creamy and homogeneous yoghurts from the shops might have either gelatine or pectin added to them. But the end product of homemade yoghurt has thin light yellow liquid layer of whey on the top of the thick curd but it tastes delicious.

If for some reason the dahi you made doesn't set, there is no need to pour it down the sink; you will be throwing away your money, time and effort. I want you to be a good and an economical house wife/husband. So here are some suggestions . . .

- ❖ Try to incubate it for a longer period in a warm place
- ❖ You can reheat the milk to lukewarm temperature (do not boil) and add another spoon of the active culture and leave it to set in the appropriate place
- ❖ If you still don't succeed, make paneer, using recipe No: 26 of this Chapter
- ❖ If it has set but it is too thin and has too much liquid, make yoghurt drink (lessee) using recipe No: 25 of this Chapter or make sauce for the pakoras curry; see recipe No: 13 of Chapter 3C.

Note to remember:

- ❖ For successful results it is important to **use any live active culture yoghurt as the starter yoghurt.**
- ❖ Try to maintain the temperature of the fermenting milk for at least the first 3-4 hours.
- ❖ Save some of the homemade dahi as starter yoghurt for the next batch.

Plain yoghurt with sugar or chopped fresh fruit or jam or marmalade:

The most in-expensive, simple, convenient and healthy snack is to take some plain yoghurt in a bowl and add some unrefined sugar to your taste or add a spoonful of jam or marmalade or some chopped fresh fruit to it and enjoy. Yoghurt with chopped fruit can be frozen to a make a healthy and delicious summer dessert or a snack.

25. Yoghurt drink (lessee)

Lessee is yoghurt diluted with water to make a drink and can be flavoured with sugar, salt, mint or fruit (consistency of lessee is thinner than a smoothie).

Sweet or salty lessee:

Serves 1-2

Ingredients:
½-1 cup of plain yoghurt
1-2 cups of water
Pinch of salt
Sugar to taste for the sweet lessee

Method:
Put everything into the blender and blend for 5-10 seconds. Pour it into a glass with a few ice cubes (optional) and enjoy this healthy drink.

Fruit lessee and yoghurt smoothie:

Fruits that can really work well in lessee are banana, raspberry, strawberry, mango and pineapple. You need to be careful how much fruit you add because the lessee can go very thick with too much fruit. However if you wish to add more fruit, it will make a good yoghurt fruit smoothie and that without doubt is a healthy snack.

Serves 1-2

Ingredients:
½-1 cup of plain yoghurt
1½-2½ cup of water
Pinch of salt
Pinch of black pepper (optional)
¼ of a banana (or fruit of your choice)
Sugar to taste

Method:
Put everything in the blender and blend for 10-15 seconds. Pour into a glass with few ice cubes (optional) and enjoy this healthy drink.

26. Paneer (Homemade cheese) snacks and how to make paneer

Paneer like cottage cheese is fresh vegetarian curd cheese; soft, light and with a refreshing taste. It can be easily made by adding any food acid like lemon juice or white vinegar or plain yoghurt to coagulate hot milk. Paneer is made by pressing out the whey from the curd, whereas the cottage cheese is eaten with the whey. Both cheeses are made without using rennet, which is an animal enzyme used in making many different types of cheese. Once it is made, store it in the fridge and use the paneer within 2-3 days. If a bigger batch is prepared, paneer is suitable for freezing. Paneer is a versatile food, so for this reason it is used in many Indian snacks, main meals and in desserts.

Preparation of homemade paneer:

Take about 500-700ml of semi-skimmed milk in a saucepan and bring to boil, and then reduce heat and slowly add 1-3 teaspoons of lemon juice/ white vinegar or even some plain yoghurt and keep stirring until all the milk is curdled. Cool it immediately either pouring some cold water to it or by adding some ice cubes. Going through this fast cooling step keeps the paneer soft for making the desserts.

Strain the coagulated milk through a very fine mesh strainer or line the strainer with a muslin/cheese cloth, then wrap the cloth tight and squeeze all the whey from the curd. Take it to the sink and wash the paneer under running tap water to remove the excessive taste of the lemon juice/vinegar. Tie the cloth tight and squeeze all the liquid from the washed curd-cheese. If all the liquid is not squeezed out, then hang it somewhere securely in the kitchen, to get rid of all the liquid from the paneer. Remove all the soft cheese from the muslin cloth into a dish. At this stage the paneer can be used as suggested in making sandwiches.

For snacks, main meals and desserts, the paneer is kneaded or rolled like dough until pliable. It can also be pressed down under heavy slab or a saucepan for a few hours. This will enable you to cut the paneer in cubes. If you want to use it for savoury dishes, before kneading or pressing down, it can be seasoned.

Paneer snacks:

Paneer sandwich:

Serves: 1-2

Ingredients:
Take 60-120g homemade paneer
1 small chopped tomato
1 chopped spring onion
¼ teaspoon of ground cumin
Red or green chilli or black pepper to your taste
Salt to taste
Some fresh water cress or chives

Method:
In a bowl put all the ingredients and blend everything with a spoon. Use this as sandwich filler in any bread of your choice.

Serving suggestions: Besides making sandwiches, serve it with a handful of chickpeas or boiled peas as a snack. Use it as a filling for the stuffed parathas and samosas, or this filling could be used in making a chapati or tortilla wraps.

Fried paneer:

Serves: 1-2

Add some butter or oil to a frying pan. Add 80-160g of paneer cubes into the hot fat and stir until it is light brown. Transfer onto the plate and splash any of the chutneys or prepare some salsa to go with it, from Chapter 6.

On the other hand, go for the simple and quick dressing of seasoned lemon juice with salt and pepper or chilli.

Paneer pakoras:

Use recipe No: 19 (pakoras) of Chapter 2 for making the batter and to fry paneer pakoras. Whatever is easiest, roll the paneer into small balls or cut into reasonable cubes and completely coat each piece of the paneer in the batter and shallow fry in the hot oil until the batter is cooked and crispy. Drain on a paper towel

Serving suggestions:
Paneer pakoras can be eaten as they are. All pickles, chutneys, and all tomato sauces can go well with the paneer pakoras.

Paneer kebab on skewer:

Paneer cubes, slices of onions, red/green peppers or aubergines or courgettes can be marinated with chicken tikka masala; use recipe No: 17 of Chapter 2. Put the marinated paneer and the vegetables on the skewers and cook, either on the coal fire or under the grill.

Serving suggestions:
Eat them as they are, or make a tortilla/chapati and paneer kebab wraps with a splash of chutney or salsa from Chapter 6.

Mutter and Paneer stir-fry: (Peas and cheese stir-fry)

Serves 1-2

Ingredients:
1-2 cups of fresh/frozen peas
60-80g paneer cubes or balls (cottage cheese is a good alternative)
1 tablespoon of tomato puree
1 teaspoon of cumin seeds
¼ teaspoon of turmeric
1 tablespoon of washed anardana (dried seeds of pomegranate—washed and soaked in hot water
1 teaspoon of ground garam masala
1 teaspoon of fresh grated or powdered ginger
1 crushed garlic clove
¼-½ teaspoon chilli powder

Some fresh coriander/water cress to garnish
Salt to taste
2 tablespoons of cooking oil of your choice
A lemon

Method:
Put 1-2 cups of fresh/frozen green peas into a colander/sieve and wash under running tap water and keep it to one side. Heat the oil in the frying pan and add the cumin seeds and stir, add all the other spices, chillies and salt to your taste and the tomato puree. Add the washed peas, mix everything and cook on medium heat for 3-4 minutes then add the paneer and simmer until the peas are cooked. Garnish with fresh coriander and a squeeze of lemon will enhance all the other flavours.

Serving suggestions:
You might like to enjoy this with some crusty bread or chapati/plain paratha, but it can be eaten on its own. It can be a good side dish with other curries.

Palak and paneer stir-fry: (Spinach and Cheese stir-fry)

Serves 1-2

Ingredients:
100-150g of chopped fresh spinach
80-100g paneer cubes or balls (cottage cheese is a good alternative)
1 small chopped onion
1 tablespoon of tomato puree
1 teaspoon of cumin seeds
¼ teaspoon of turmeric
1 teaspoon of lemon juice
1 teaspoon of sesame seeds
1 crushed garlic clove
¼ teaspoon chilli powder or black pepper
Salt to taste
1 tablespoon of cooking oil of your choice
A lemon

Method:
Wash and chop the fresh spinach and keep it to one side. Heat the oil in the frying pan and soften the chopped onions. Then add the cumin and the sesame seeds and stir for 1-2 seconds. Add all the other spices, tomato puree and chillies and salt to your taste and stir all the ingredients together. Add paneer and the chopped spinach and then mix everything with a splash of lemon juice and cook on the medium heat for 2-3 minutes.

Serving suggestions:
You might like to enjoy with some crusty bread or chapati/plain paratha but it can be eaten on its own. It can be a good side dish with other curries.

27. Indian Soups

A. *Lentil and rice soup*

Serves 2-3

Ingredients:
1 cup of red lentils
2-3 tablespoons of rice
1 small chopped onion
1 medium chopped tomato
½ teaspoon of crushed ginger
1-2 cloves of garlic
1^{inch}of cinnamon stick or ¼ teaspoon of ground cinnamon
1 teaspoon of cumin seeds
1 teaspoon of ground coriander
1-2 whole black cloves
3-4 black peppercorns
1 small whole green chilli (It gives a good chilli smell and a good chilli flavour without making the soup chilli hot)
Salt to taste

Note to remember: Addition of any vegetable will make the soup even more wholesome and substantial.

Method:
Before cooking, make sure you always wash the lentils and rice in a sieve, under running tap water. This should get rid of any dust and grit. Put the washed lentils and rice in a suitable pan and add all the other ingredients. Add about 4 cups of water, bring it to the boil and then continue to cook on a medium heat until the lentils and rice are cooked. Add more water if you prefer a thinner soup and dry the liquid if you are fond of thick soup. Alternatively, if you like the smooth texture of soup, pass the soup through a blender, when it is cooled to room temperature. (Before blending just take out the whole spices and the chilli). Season the soup with salt according to your taste.

Serving suggestions:
When serving, add a tablespoon of plain yoghurt to the soup. On its own it is a good starter or a healthy snack but it can also be eaten with any type of bread including all Indian breads.

B.   *Beans soup*
Use the lentil and rice soup recipe by using a mixture of several beans or using any one type of bean with some suitable vegetables. The suggested vegetables are onions, carrots, celery sticks and potatoes. It is best to soak the beans overnight and when cooked pass through the blender. (Before blending just take out the whole spices and the chilli). Season the soup with salt according to your taste.

Serving suggestions:
When serving, add 1 tablespoon of plain yoghurt to the soup. On its own it is a good starter or a healthy snack but it can also be eaten with any type of bread including all Indian breads.

C.   *Vegetable soup*

Serves 2-3

Ingredients:
1 large chopped onion
2 medium chopped tomatoes
1 peeled and chopped carrots
2 florets of cauliflower

2 chopped celery sticks
½ cup of sweet corn
¼ cup of peas
1 large potato
½ teaspoon of crushed ginger and
1-2 cloves of garlic
1^{inch}of cinnamons stick
1 teaspoon of cumin seeds
1 teaspoon of ground coriander
1-2 whole black cloves
3-4 black peppercorns
Salt to taste

1 small whole green chilli (It gives a good chilli smell and a good chilli flavour without making the soup chilli hot)

Method:
In a suitable saucepan, place all the washed and chopped vegetables along with all the spices. Add about 4 cups of water, bring it to the boil and then continue to cook on medium heat until the vegetables are cooked. It tastes good whether you have clear soup with the chunks of vegetable or all the vegetables and the liquid are blended together. Before blending remove the whole spices and the chilli. Season the soup with salt according to your taste.

Serving suggestions:
When serving if you prefer, add a tablespoon of plain yoghurt. On its own it is good starter or a healthy snack but it can also be eaten with any type of bread including all Indian breads.

D. *Chicken and vegetable soup*

Serves 2-3

Ingredients:
Select either 2 skinned chicken thighs or drumsticks, or the wings, neck of the chicken, the backbone and rib cage.
1 large chopped onion
2 medium chopped tomatoes
1-2 peeled and chopped carrots

½ cup of sweet corn
¼ cup of peas
2 chopped celery sticks
1 large potato
½ teaspoon of crushed ginger and
2-3 cloves of garlic
1^{inch} of cinnamons stick
1 teaspoon of cumin seeds
1-2 whole black cloves
3-4 black peppercorns
1 small whole green chilli (It gives a good chilli smell and a good chilli flavour without making the soup chilli hot)
Salt to taste

Method:
In a suitable saucepan, place all the washed and the chopped vegetables and at least two chicken pieces of your choice with all the spices. Add about 4 cups of water, bring it to boil and then continue to cook on medium heat until the vegetables and the chicken are cooked. It tastes good whether you have clear soup with the chunks of the vegetable and the chicken, or all the vegetables, meat and the liquid are blended together. Before blending discard the cinnamon stick, the chilli and the bones after taking the meat from them. Season the soup with salt according to your taste.

Serving suggestions:
When serving if you prefer, add a tablespoon of plain yoghurt. On its own it is a good starter or a healthy snack but it can also be eaten with any type of bread including all Indian breads.

Chapter 3

Main Meals

Note to remember: Please go through the recipes cautiously to check if you are sensitive or intolerant to any of the ingredients and make sure to eliminate or to use a suitable alternative.

3A. Preparation of the basic curry sauce

Curry recipes are easy to learn and once you master the basic curry sauce it will help you to make several different curries. Note that the thickness/ consistency of the sauce is not made with the addition of the flour, but using appropriate amounts of onions, tomatoes, plain yoghurt, ground coriander, cumin and the paste of ginger and garlic. Cooking curries is easier these days as food stores have cubes of frozen crushed garlic and the ginger. The whole and ground spices are easily available in packs of all sizes.

Ingredients:
2 finely chopped large onions
½-1 tin of tomatoes (tin of 400g)
4-5 cloves of crushed garlic or 1 frozen cube or 1-2 teaspoon of garlic puree
1 tablespoon of crushed fresh ginger or 1 frozen cube
2 tablespoons of ground coriander
1 teaspoon of cumin seeds
1 tablespoon of garam masala
¾ teaspoon of turmeric powder
½-1 teaspoon of red chilli powder (do add a bit more if you enjoy chilli-hot food)

1-2 bay leaves or curry leaves
½ teaspoon of salt
2-3 tablespoons of cooking oil of your choice

Method:
In a suitable saucepan add the cooking oil and on a medium heat fry onions until golden-brown; lower the heat or if preferred take the pan off the heat. The oil will still be hot enough to fry the spices, so add all the spices and stir for 3-4 seconds. Add rest of the ingredients including salt and put the pan back on the hob. Stir well to give a good mix and add about ½ cup of water. Cover the pan with the lid. On a medium heat, further cook the sauce and keep stirring from time to time. The cooked sauce should look like a smooth and homogeneous mixture. This sauce should be sufficient to make curry with 500-700g of meat/fish/vegetables.

Note to remember:

- This sauce can be used for making many types of curries, but use the curry sauce in proportion to the quantity of meat or vegetables.
- The left over curry sauce can be used for making another dish or freeze until you need it again.
- This is also a flavouring curry sauce which can be used to give a delicate flavour to all types of meats, fish, vegetables, soups, beans and all daal dishes.
- For convenience, you can prepare the curry sauce in advance and refrigerate it or freeze it.
- Basic curry sauce has only half a teaspoon of salt so further addition of some more salt is required in all the dishes you prepare with this curry sauce.

Please note that not all recipes require the basic curry sauce; e.g. Korma, Pasanda, meat/vegetable stir-fry, vegetables and pakoras curry dishes have their own unique cooking sauces. To get good results please follow the recipes which are provided.

3B. Meat Curries

1. Lamb curry

Serves 4-6

Ingredients:
Chopped lamb shoulder/leg. Reasonably sized pieces (about 500-700g)
Use recipe A from Chapter 3 to prepare the curry sauce.

Method:
Wash the meat in the colander, drain the water and add to the curry sauce. Put the pan on a medium heat and give it a good mix. Cover the pan with the lid and cook the meat for about 3-4 minutes. Don't forget to stir it frequently. Then add about 2 cups of water, put the lid on the pan and continue to cook on fairly high heat until the meat is tender. Traditionally this dish has a thick sauce. Garnish with a handful of freshly chopped coriander or you can use a smaller amount of chopped fresh basil or parsley.

Serving suggestions:
Serve with rice or any Indian bread from Chapter 5, accompanied by plain yoghurt, or any raita or any of the fresh chutneys from Chapter 6 of the condiments.

2. Goshtt aloo (Lamb curry with potatoes or turnips or pumpkin or peas)

Serves 4-6

Ingredients:
Chopped lamb shoulder/leg. Reasonably sized pieces (400-500g)
4-6 medium potatoes (use potatoes that will not go mushy)
Use recipe A from Chapter 3 to prepare the curry sauce.

Method:
Wash the meat in the colander and drain the water. Add it to the curry sauce that you have already prepared using the curry sauce recipe. Cook the meat for about 3-4 minutes on medium heat. Don't forget to stir

it frequently. Add 3 cups of water, put the lid on the pan and continue to cook for 15 minutes or until the meat is almost cooked. Then add 4 medium peeled potatoes cut into medium size chunks. At this stage if the sauce runs too dry then add another cup of hot water. Continue to cook until the meat and the potatoes are well cooked. Traditionally the sauce of this well-known dish is fairly runny. Garnish with fresh chopped coriander or alternatively you can use fresh basil or parsley.

Serving suggestions:
Serve with rice or any Indian bread from Chapter 5, accompanied by plain yoghurt, or any raita or any of the fresh chutneys from Chapter 6 of the condiments.

3. Sabzi Goshtt (Vegetables & meat curry)

Any of the following vegetables can be cooked with lamb or beef or chicken to make a dry curry with—okras, cauliflower, cabbage, courgettes, green/red peppers, runner beans, fine green beans, carrots, potatoes, peas and aubergines.

Serves 4-6

Ingredients:
Chopped lamb shoulder/leg. Reasonably sized pieces (400-600g)
Florets of a large cauliflower
Use recipe A from Chapter 3 to prepare the curry sauce.

Method:
Wash the meat in the colander and drain the water. Add it to the curry sauce that you have already prepared using the curry sauce recipe. Cook the meat for about 3-4 minutes on medium heat. Don't forget to stir it frequently. Add about 1-1½ cups of water, put the lid on the pan and continue to cook until the meat is almost cooked. Then add small florets of the cauliflower. Stir to mix the cauliflower and the meat. Continue to cook until the meat and the vegetables are well cooked and all the liquid has dried. Traditionally it is a dry curry; that means it is moist but not with a runny sauce. Garnish with fresh chopped coriander or alternatively you can use a small amount of fresh basil or parsley.

Serving suggestions:
Serve with rice or any Indian bread from Chapter 5, accompanied by plain yoghurt, or any raita or any of the fresh chutneys from Chapter 6 of the condiments.

4.   Stir fry liver

Serves: 1-2

Ingredients:
50-100g diced liver of your choice
½ teaspoon of crushed ginger
1 small green chilli finely chopped
1 teaspoon of garam masala
¼ teaspoon of turmeric
¼ teaspoon of red chilli
Black pepper, tip of a teaspoon
1 large onion finely chopped
1 medium chopped tomato or ½-1 tablespoon of tin/puree tomato
½ teaspoon of crushed garlic
2 tablespoons of cooking oil
Fresh chopped coriander or water cress
Salt to taste

Note to remember:

❖ Before dicing the liver, try to remove all the hard connective tissue by using a knife or a pair of kitchen scissors.
❖ If possible remove/peel any outer thin membrane using your hands.
❖ Liver which is sold in big slices needs to be diced or cut into small pieces with a sharp knife for stir fry.
❖ Keep in mind that over cooking and overheating hardens the liver.

Method:
In a suitable frying pan, sauté the finely chopped onion in the cooking oil of your choice. Stir in all the other ingredients except the liver (do not forget to season with salt). Cook for 40-60 seconds and then add the diced liver and stir fry over fairly high heat for 1-2 minutes. When cooked, immediately take it off the heat and serve it straight away as reheating hardens the liver.

Serving suggestions:
Serve with rice or chapati or naan/pitta bread, plain paratha or with any other bread from Chapter 5.

If preferred, pass the stir-fried liver through a food processor to make a coarse paste (pâté) and use it as sandwich filler. However you choose to eat the tender and the delicious liver, remember to add some green salad.

5.   Meat and spinach curry (Goshtt and saag)

Serves 4-6

Spinach is used in many vegetable and meat dishes and is also a common ingredient in the preparation of pakoras. *Saag is the combination of different greens cooked together and spinach is the main part to make the saag.* Goshtt and saag is served on weddings and celebration parties. But it is also served regularly in most of the Indian restaurants, too.

Traditionally the lamb/mutton is used in this dish but beef, chicken or turkey works as good as the lamb.

Preparation of the spinach saag:

Ingredients:
Spinach either fresh 600-800g or frozen 300-500g
3-4 sprigs of broccoli
1 handful of Brussels sprouts
1-2 whole medium chillies
1 handful of fresh or dried methi leaves, if available

Method:
Wash spinach, broccoli, Brussels sprouts, methi and green chilli. Put them all in a suitable pan and cook for 15-20 minutes on medium heat with a splash of water. Take it off the heat and let it cool. Then pass the cooked spinach mixture through a food processor just to break the stringy stalks of the greens and to homogenise into a coarse puree.

Preparation of the curry:

Ingredients:
Chopped lamb shoulder or leg pieces (400-500g)
Use recipe A from Chapter 3 to prepare the curry sauce and use it all.

Method:
Wash the meat in the colander, drain the water and add it to the curry sauce that you have already prepared. Cook the meat for about 3-4 minutes on medium heat. Don't forget to stir it frequently. Add 1-2 cup of water, put the lid on the pan and continue to cook on medium heat until the meat is tender and all the liquid is dried. Now add the prepared and cooked spinach mixture into the cooked lamb, give a good mix with the wooden spoon and simmer it on the low heat for further 10-15 minutes.

Serving suggestions:
Serve with rice or any Indian bread from Chapter 5, accompanied by plain yoghurt or any of the raitas or with any of the green chutney mixed in the plain yoghurt. To lift the taste of this dish, use the salsa recipe, No: 8 of Chapter 6.

6.   Chicken curry

Serves 3-4

Ingredients:
Skinned portions of chicken thighs and drumsticks (6-8 pieces)
Or; chicken breast 3-5, reasonable size pieces
Use recipe A from Chapter 3 to prepare the curry sauce.

Method:
Wash the meat in the colander, drain the water and add it to the curry sauce that you have already prepared. Cook the meat for about 3-4 minutes on medium heat. Don't forget to stir it frequently. Add 2 cups of water, put the lid on the pan and continue to cook until the meat is tender. Traditionally the sauce of this dish is fairly thick. To make the sauce thicker just increase the heat. To make the sauce runny add more hot water. Any vegetable can be added to the chicken as in recipe No: 2 of Chapter 3B of lamb cooked with the potatoes. Garnish with freshly chopped coriander or alternatively use smaller amounts of fresh basil or parsley.

Serving suggestions:
Serve with rice or any Indian bread from Chapter 5, accompanied by plain yoghurt or any raitas or any of the fresh chutneys from Chapter 6 of the condiments.

7.   Meat and lentil curry (Goshtt and daal)

7A. *Mutton or lamb or chicken and chana daal curry:*

Goshtt and daal is a proper and well known Punjabi dish. Mutton and Chana daal are the common ingredients used. Some people prefer oxtail, lamb shanks. Neck and short ribs can also work in this dish. But there is no reason why beef or chicken can't be used. I prefer red/green lentils or skinned and spilt moong daal with skinned chicken thighs/ drum sticks. Most of the recipes use chana daal, but all the lentils can be used and they all make this dish as good as with the latter.

Note to remember: During the process of cooking, the meat can be overcooked or come off the bones. So if you prefer that the meat is cooked and also stays on the bone, cook the lentils separately and then add to the meat. Then all you need to do is to mix the cooked daal and the cooked meat together and on low heat simmer it so that the lentils will absorb the all the flavours of the meat curry. If you choose meat like oxtail, neck or shank you can save energy by using a crockpot (slow cooker) or a pressure cooker.

Preparation of mutton and chana daal:

Serves 3-5

Ingredients:
Mutton 250-300g (Cut into reasonably sized pieces)
1-2 cups of chana daal (washed and soaked in warm water)
1 chopped large onion
1 chopped large fresh tomato or 1-2 tablespoons of tomato puree
3-4 cloves of crushed garlic or 1 frozen cube or a teaspoon of garlic puree
1 tablespoon of crushed fresh ginger or 1 frozen cube
2 tablespoons of ground coriander
1 tablespoon of ground cumin/cumin seeds

1 tablespoon of garam masala
1 teaspoon of turmeric powder
1 teaspoon of mustard seeds
1 teaspoon of red chilli powder (do add bit more if you enjoy chilli-hot food)
1-2 bay leaves or curry leaves
2-3 tablespoons of cooking oil of your choice
Salt to taste
Chopped fresh coriander (handful), 1 teaspoon of shredded ginger and 1 chopped green chilli for garnishing.

Method:
In a suitable pan put 2-3 tablespoons of cooking oil and on medium heat fry the chopped onion and then add all the other spices. Stir it for a minute and then add the mutton and keep stirring for another 2 minutes. Add about 3 cups of water and then add the chana daal, stir well and put the lid on the pan. Continue to cook on high heat for 5 minutes and then turn it down to medium heat. Cook until both the meat and the daal is cooked. Put it in a serving dish and garnish with fresh coriander, ½ teaspoon of chopped green chillies and a teaspoon of shredded/grated fresh ginger.

Serving suggestions:
Serve with rice or any Indian bread from Chapter 5, accompanied by plain yoghurt, or any raitas or any of the fresh chutneys, salsa and pickles from Chapter 6 of the condiments. A squeeze of lemon for the daal dishes is recommended.

7B. *Chicken and the skinned spilt moong daal curry:*

Serves: 3-6

Ingredients:
Chicken 6-8 washed, skinned drum sticks or thighs
2 cups of skinned spilt moong daal (washed and soaked in warm water)
1chopped large onion
1 chopped large fresh tomato or 1-2 tablespoons of tomato puree
4-5 cloves of crushed garlic or 1 frozen cube or a teaspoon full of garlic puree
1 tablespoon of crushed fresh ginger or 1 frozen cube
2 tablespoons of ground coriander
1 tablespoon of ground cumin or cumin seeds

1 tablespoon of garam masala
1 teaspoon of turmeric powder
1 teaspoon of mustard seeds
¾ teaspoon of red chilli powder (do add bit more if you enjoy chilli-hot food)
1-2 bay leaves or curry leaves
Salt to taste
2-3 tablespoons of cooking oil of your choice
Chopped fresh coriander (handful), a teaspoon of shredded ginger and a chopped green chilli for garnishing

Method:
In a suitable pan put 3-4 tablespoons of cooking oil and on medium heat fry the chopped onion and then add all the other spices. Stir it for a minute and then add the chicken and keep stirring for another 2 minutes. Add the moong daal and then add about 2-3 cups of water and stir well. Put the lid on the pan, continue to cook on high heat for 5 minutes and then turn it down to a medium heat. Cook until both the meat and the daal is cooked. Put it in a serving dish and garnish with fresh coriander, ½ teaspoon of chopped green chillies and a teaspoon of shredded/grated fresh ginger.

Serving suggestions:
Serve with rice or any Indian bread from Chapter 5, accompanied by plain yoghurt with chopped cucumber. Green chutneys, plain yoghurt and pickles are popular condiments used with all the daal dishes. A squeeze of a lemon for the daal dishes is recommended, too.

8.   Chicken and vegetable stir-fry

Serves 2-3

Ingredients:
Chicken breasts1-2, reasonable size pieces (marinate the chicken with 1-2 tablespoons of plain yoghurt, salt and pepper)
2 cups of frozen mixed vegetables
1 medium chopped onion
1 medium chopped fresh tomato (tin/pureed tomatoes can be used)
Garlic and ginger to taste
1teaspoon of cumin seeds
Salt and chilli to taste

Method:
Fry the chopped onions in cooking oil and stir fry the chicken pieces for 2-3 minutes on high heat. Carefully take out the chicken and in the same fat cook the vegetable for 1-2 minutes and then add the rest of the ingredients. Stir everything together with few splashes of water and cover the pan until the vegetables are almost done. Put the chicken back into the vegetable pan; simmer it for another 2-3 minutes on low heat. Garnish with fresh coriander or small amount of chopped curly parsley.

Serving suggestions:
Serve with rice or any Indian bread from Chapter 5, accompanied by plain yoghurt. This can be also be used in making the tortilla/chapati/paratha wraps with the salsa (see Chapter 6).

9.   Beef curry with potatoes or turnips or Kadoo (pumpkins) or peas

Serves 3-4

Ingredients:
About 300-400g of beef chopped into reasonably sized pieces
4-5 medium turnips peeled, chopped and cooked in water, ready to go into the meat

Use recipe A from Chapter 3 to prepare the curry sauce and use as much as required in proportion to the amount of the ingredients you are cooking. Note that you have the option or the control to use as much sauce in the curry as you prefer.

Method:
Add the chopped beef to the curry sauce that you have already prepared, using the curry sauce recipe. Cook the meat for about 3-4 minutes on medium heat. Don't forget to stir it frequently. Add 3 cups of water, put the lid on the pan and continue to cook for at least 15 minutes or until the meat is almost cooked. Then add the cooked turnips to the meat and further cook for another 5 minutes with the meat. Unlike potatoes the turnips give a good taste when they go mushy, whereas the mushy potatoes ruin the taste of the sauce. Traditionally the sauce of this dish is fairly thick. A squeeze of lemon enhances the taste of the cooked turnips and garnish with chopped fresh coriander.

Serving suggestions:
Serve with rice or any Indian bread from Chapter 5, accompanied by plain yoghurt, or any raitas or any of the fresh chutneys from Chapter 6 of the condiments

10. Fish curry

Serves 3-4

Ingredients:
Fillets of any fish can be used for making the fish curry (4-6 fillets).

Prepare the fish by washing with the turmeric water (just add ½ teaspoon of turmeric powder to 300ml of water, turmeric will take some of the strong smell of the fish) and drain it well. Cut the washed fillets into decent sized pieces.

Use recipe A from Chapter 3 to prepare the curry sauce and use as much as required in proportion to the amount of fish you are cooking. Work out by weighing the fish.

Method:
Place the washed and well drained fish in the curry sauce. Mix it gently and simmer with ½ cup of water until the fish is cooked. Garnish with fresh chopped coriander and alternatively you can use fresh basil or parsley.

Serving suggestions:
Serve with rice or any Indian bread from Chapter 5. Lime pickle or any green chutney will be a good accompaniment to this dish.

Korma

Korma is one of the curries, when the meat or the vegetables are slowly stewed with minimum liquid (water) and dahi (plain yoghurt). It used to be a prestigious and rich dish which was served in the Mughal royal courts, and was called Shahi (royal) Korma. This was not a common every day dish but korma nowadays is served in all the restaurants seven days a week and frequently cooked at home.

Note to remember:

❖ Cooking with yoghurt is tricky because it can easily separate into curd and whey.

❖ Using the full fat yoghurt can help to avoid that.

❖ Try not to use it straight from the fridge but remember to take it out to reach room temperature.

❖ Remove the pan from the hob and let it cool before adding yoghurt.

❖ Add yoghurt gradually; mix it well with meat/vegetable.

❖ Cover the pan first with cooking foil and then put the lid over the foil to keep all the moisture in.

11. Meat korma

Serves 4-6

Ingredients:
400g-500g of washed and drained boneless lamb or chicken or beef pieces
2 large chopped onions
1 tablespoon of garam masala
2 tablespoons of ground coriander
¼ teaspoon of turmeric
½ teaspoon of red chillies
2 teaspoons of desiccated coconut or 2 tablespoons of coconut milk
1 tablespoon of grounded poppy seeds or 1 tablespoon of grounded almonds
1 cup of plain yoghurt
2 small green chillies
2-3 whole green cardamoms
1-2 black cloves
Fresh chopped ginger, about 1 tablespoon
1-2 teaspoons crushed garlic
Salt to taste
A handful of fresh coriander for garnishing
Cooking oil

Method:
In a suitable bowl put all the ingredients except the yoghurt and the chopped onions. Mix it well so that all the meat is coated with the spices. Marinate for at least for an hour. Fry the chopped onions in 3-4 tablespoons of oil in

suitable saucepan until light brown. Reduce the heat and add the marinated meat and keep stirring on a medium heat for 3-4 minutes or until the meat is brown. Take the pan off the heat and let it cool before adding the plain yoghurt as at a high temperature the yoghurt will separate from its liquid. When the meat is slightly cooler (from hot to warm) add half of the yoghurt and mix it well with the meat. Mix it thoroughly and put it back on the medium heat. Cover the pan with a lid. Continue cooking for 4-5 minutes. Take the pan off the heat and let it cool (from hot to warm) before adding rest of the yoghurt. Add the remaining yoghurt, mixing it thoroughly and put it back on the medium heat. Cover the pan with a lid (to keep the moisture in) until the meat is cooked and the remaining sauce is very thick but moist. (Moisten the meat with very little boiled water if it runs too dry). Garnish with fresh coriander.

Serving suggestions:
Serve with rice or any Indian bread from Chapter 5. Mixed pickle or any fresh chutney will enhance the taste of the korma dish

12. Koffata (Meatball) curry

Meatball is a truly universal dish, made from ground/mincemeat, hand rolled and cooked either by frying or baking or by steaming or braising in a sauce. There is variety of meat that can be used in the preparation of meatballs but the most popular meat used is lamb and beef.

So here is a recipe of making a delicious Indian meatball curry.

Serves 4-6

Ingredients:
400-500g of lamb or beef or chicken or turkey mince
1 large chopped onion
1 teaspoon of garam masala
1 tablespoon of ground coriander
¼ teaspoon of turmeric
½ teaspoon of red chillies
1-2 tablespoons of desiccated coconut
1 tablespoon of ground poppy seeds or ground almonds
1 tablespoon of ground ginger or fresh grated ginger

Handful of fresh coriander
Handful of chopped leaves of fresh leaves of spinach
3 small green chillies
1 egg for binding the meat

Method:
Pass all the ingredients including the meat and salt through a food processor to make a homogeneous mixture. Take the mixture out and roll it into small balls and deep/shallow fry until light brown. Put them on a paper towel to get rid of the excess fat.

Or . . . *(use this method if you want to reduce the content of the fat in the meat)* Roll the mixture into small balls and put them carefully into a pan of hot water. Cook them for 10-15 minutes on high heat and then take them out. Either discard the liquid or use it in the next step of the cooking by removing the fat.

At room temperature the animal fat becomes semi-solid and can be easily removed and discarded. So leave the liquid to cool, you will notice that the semi-solid fat sets on the top. Take a spoon and remove the fat and discard it. *This fat free liquid can be used for the further cooking of the meatball curry.

Make the curry sauce by using recipe A of Chapter 3 and put the fried/boiled meatballs into it. Cook the meatballs in the curry sauce for about 3-4 minutes on medium heat. Don't forget to stir it frequently. At this stage add any vegetable you prefer. Add 2-3 cups of water or * the fat free liquid (kept from the previous step) put the lid on the pan and cook on medium heat for 15-20 minutes, but make sure that the meat is cooked.

Traditionally the sauce of this dish is of medium-runny consistency. Garnish with fresh chopped coriander and alternatively you can use fresh basil or parsley.

Serving suggestions:
Serve with rice or chapati or naan/pitta bread, plain paratha, accompanied by plain yoghurt or any raita or any of the green chutneys.

Note of suggestion: Reduce the liquid of the meatball curry sauce and you can serve with cooked spaghettis or pastas. You can also cook potatoes or peas or turnips or aubergines with the meatball curry, as in recipes No: 2 and No: 9 of Chapter 3B—this adds more taste and goodness to the meatball curry.

13. Keema Chawal (Mincemeat and rice), see recipe No: 4 of Chapter 4

14. Mincemeat with potato and peas (keema, Aloo and mutter curry)

Serves 3-4

Mincemeat can also create good dishes with cauliflower, cabbage, courgettes, red/green peppers and aubergines. Use the same recipe as of mincemeat, potato and peas.

Ingredients:
250-300g of lamb or beef or turkey or chicken mince
2-3 medium sized chopped onions
1 tablespoon of garam masala
1 tablespoon of ground coriander
1 teaspoon of cumin seed
½ teaspoon of turmeric
1 teaspoon of red chillies
Fresh chopped ginger, about a tablespoon
Crushed garlic, or a tablespoon of garlic paste
1 small green chilli
½-1 tin of tomatoes
Chunks of 4-6 medium peeled potatoes
1 cup of frozen or fresh peas
Salt to taste
1-2 tablespoons of cooking oil
Fresh coriander for garnishing

Method:
In a suitable cooking pan, fry the chopped onions in a small amount (two tablespoon) of cooking oil of your choice. Add all the spices—ginger, garlic, tomatoes and some salt; keep stirring the mixture. Then add the mincemeat and fry with all the ingredients for 3-5 minutes. At this stage

add the potatoes and the peas with 1½ cups of water, put the lid on the pan and continue to cook until all ingredients are well cooked and all liquid is dried. It should be a dry curry which means there should not be runny sauce. For garnishing: chop some onion, a small green chilli and fresh coriander and a squeeze of lemon juice.

Serving suggestions:
Serve with rice or chapati or naan/pitta bread, plain paratha, accompanied by plain yoghurt, or any raita or any of the fresh chutneys from Chapter 6 of the condiments

Note to remember: *If you prefer more peas and fewer potatoes, or a little less meat and more of the vegetables, it is your meal and you should enjoy your preferred quantities of the main ingredients. All other ingredients will be sufficient but do check if the dish has enough salt and chilli.*

15. Chicken tikka masala (Also see recipe No: 17 of Chapter 2)

Serves 2-4

Ingredients:
2-3 chicken breasts (cut into reasonably sized pieces.)
3 tablespoons of plain yoghurts
1 teaspoon of paprika
½ teaspoon of chilli powder
1 teaspoon of garam masala
1 teaspoon of ground coriander
1 teaspoon of ground cumin
1 teaspoon of ground fresh or ginger powder, 1-2 cloves of garlic and 1medium onion (blend the three ingredients into a paste, using the food processor)
Fresh coriander for the garnish
Salt to taste
2-3 tablespoons of cooking oil

Method:
Put the yoghurt, the spices and salt into a bowl and mix everything. Then add the chicken pieces and stir it so that all the chicken is coated with the yoghurt mixture. Leave it in the fridge for 2-3 hours. In a frying pan put

2-3 tablespoons of cooking oil and put it on a high heat. In the hot oil, gently put the marinated pieces of chicken. Keep stirring and fry it for about 2 minutes. If the chicken is not cooked, then cook it bit longer. Take the chicken tikka out and place into the serving dish and garnish with fresh coriander and a squeeze of lemon.

Serving suggestions:
It is a good starter, either to be eaten on its own or with the yoghurt chutneys or with pickles. It is a good accompaniment to vegetable pasta, couscous, vegetable rice or noodles. It is also a good additional dish with the lentils and vegetable curries. Chicken tikka with salad can make good tortilla /chapati/paratha wrap.

16. Tandoori chicken (Also see recipe No: 18 of Chapter 2)

Serves 3-4

Ingredients:
6-8 skinned chicken drum sticks or chicken thighs
3 tablespoons of plain yoghurt
3 teaspoons of paprika
1 teaspoon of chilli powder
1 teaspoon of garam masala
2 teaspoons of ground coriander
1 teaspoon of ground fresh or ginger powder
1 tablespoon of lemon juice
Salt to taste

Method:
Wash and dry the chicken pieces and place into a suitable bowl. Mix the yoghurt with all the other ingredients and pour it over the chicken. Stir well so that chicken is coated with the mixture. Leave the chicken to marinate in the fridge overnight or for at least 4-5 hours. Preheat the oven at 180°C/355°F/Gas mark 4. Line the oven tray with the cooking oil before putting the chicken on it. Cover the chicken with the foil and place the tray in the preheated oven. After 40-45 minutes, take off the foil, turn over each piece and continue to cook until the chicken is thoroughly done. Take the tandoori chicken out and keep it warm by covering it with foil.

Serving suggestions:
Tandoori chicken is a good starter, either to be eaten on its own or with yoghurt chutneys or with pickles. It is a good accompaniment to vegetable pasta, couscous, vegetable rice or noodles. It is also a good additional dish with lentils or vegetable curries. The meat from the tandoori chicken with salad greens or salsa is suitable for making chapati or paratha or tortilla wraps.

17. What else can you make with a whole chicken?
Besides roasting a whole chicken, you can also make a good use of different portions of a whole fresh chicken to make quite a few dishes; using the recipes given in this book. For example you can make a chicken curry (recipe No: 6 of Chapter 3B) **or** tandoori chicken (recipe No: 16 of Chapter 3B) from the leg and wing portions. Use the chicken breast to make Chicken tikka masala **or** to make a stir fry dish with vegetables (recipe No: 15 and No: 8 of Chapter 3B). You are now left with the neck, backbone and rib cage. These can be used in making chicken and the vegetable soup (recipe No: 27D of Chapter 2). *This way nothing is wasted; a variety of five dishes can be prepared and consequently using the whole chicken gives you good value for your money.*

18. Beef or lamb Pasanda
The name of the dish "Pasanda" is taken from the Urdu/Hindi word *pasand* meaning the favourite/selected/liked/preferred. It is a mild hot dish in a creamy sauce. The Pasanda dish is made from the beef/lamb undercut meat. The meat is beaten with wooden meat hammer and then cut into pieces about 2 inches in size.

For Marinade:

Ingredients:
500g good quality beef or lamb (each piece about 2 inches in size)
½ cup of natural yoghurt
1 tablespoon coriander powder
1 teaspoon Garam Masala
½ teaspoon turmeric powder
¼ teaspoon chilli powder
1 teaspoon paprika powder for colour
1 chopped small green chilli
1 medium onion, peeled and grated or very finely chopped

3 small cloves garlic, peeled and grated
2 inches of ginger, peeled and grated
2 tablespoons ground almonds
Salt to taste

Method:
Prepare the marinade by making the puree of garlic, onion and ginger by using the blender. Take out all the puree and put into a suitable bowl. Add the yoghurt and rest of the ingredients and mix it well. Put the meat pieces in the mixture and stir well so that the meat is coated with the mixture. Leave it to marinate in the fridge overnight or for at least 4-5 hours.

For cooking:

Ingredients:
1 large onion, peeled and finely chopped
1 teaspoon cumin seeds
½ teaspoon of fresh or dry methi leaves
2-3 black cardamoms
2-3 green cardamoms
2-3 bay leaves
1-2 ^{inches} of cinnamon sticks
3-4 cloves
½ cup water
2-3 tablespoons cooking oil
A handful of chopped coriander leaves

Method:
In a suitable pan fry the chopped onions in cooking oil, add all the spices and stir until cumin seeds start to pop. Then put the marinated meat with all the marinade and mix it well with all the roasted spices. Reduce the heat, put the lid on the pan and continue to cook with ½ a cup of water until the meat is cooked. Remember to stir the meat from time to time. Make sure that most of the liquid is absorbed and the meat is in a moist and thick creamy sauce. Garnish with fresh chopped coriander.

Serving suggestions:
Pasanda dish can be served with rice or any Indian bread from Chapter 5.

19. Nargisi Koffata curry

Serves 3-4

Ingredients:
300-500g of lamb or beef or chicken or turkey mince
4-6 large eggs boiled and shelled
1 finely chopped spring onion
1 teaspoon of garam masala
1 teaspoon of ground coriander
¼ teaspoon of turmeric
¼ teaspoon of red chillies
1 teaspoon of ground poppy seeds or ground almonds
1 teaspoon of fresh ground /grated ginger
1 handful of fresh coriander
1 handful of finely chopped fresh spinach leaves
1 small green chilli
1 egg for binding the meat

Method:
Pass all the ingredients including the meat through a food processor to make a homogeneous mixture. Take the mixture out and encase each boiled egg with the meat mixture.

How to shape the Nargisi koffata:
Divide the meat mixture into 4-6 equal portions. On a sheet of greased proof paper (or use a sheet of food wrap film greased with oil) take a portion of the meat mixture and flatten into an oblong shape about 5×3 inches using your hand. Place the boiled and shelled egg in the centre. Bring all the sides of the paper/food wrap film towards the centre to encase the egg. Using your hands, smooth the meat mixture around the egg and press the edges. Repeat encasing the other eggs with meat.

How to cook the Nargisi koffata:
Fry the koffatas in small amount of fat, until they are cooked and are light brown. Take them out and put them on a paper towel to get rid of the excess fat. The koffatas, when thoroughly cooked can be a good snack (See recipe No: 16 in Chapter 2). But koffatas when cooked in the curry sauce become a main meal dish.

Make the curry sauce by using recipe A from Chapter 3, and put the fried nargisi koffatas into it. Add ½ cup of water to the sauce and, put the lid on the pan and cook on medium heat for 4-5 minutes. Traditionally the consistency of the sauce is very thick. When dishing out, put all the sauce first in the serving dish. Use a sharp knife to cut each koffata into two halves. Put them on the top of the sauce with the yoke side up. Garnish with fresh chopped coriander or alternatively you can use fresh basil or parsley.

Serving suggestions:
Serve with rice or any Indian bread from Chapter 5, accompanied by plain yoghurt or any riata or any of the green chutneys.

3C. Vegetarian curries

1. Potatoes, peas and carrots curry (or frozen mixed vegetable)

Serves 2-3

Ingredients:
3-4 medium peeled potatoes cut in small chunks
2-3 carrots peeled and diced.
1-2 cups of frozen peas or 1 cup of frozen mixed vegetables
1 chopped large onion
1 fresh tomato or 1 tablespoon of tomato puree
½ teaspoon of garlic
½ teaspoon of ginger
¼ teaspoon of turmeric
½ teaspoon of red chilli powder or 1 teaspoon of paprika
1 teaspoon of cumin seeds
1 teaspoon of garam masala
Salt to taste
3-4 tablespoons of cooking oil of your choice
Fresh coriander for garnishing

Method:
Heat the cooking oil in a pan and fry the chopped onions until golden-brown. Add the spices, ginger, garlic and the tomato. Stir for 10-20 seconds and then add the potato chunks and other vegetables. Stir to mix everything

and add ½ a cup of water; put the lid on the pan and continue to cook. Take the pan off the heat when vegetables are cooked and all the liquid is dried. Garnish with chopped fresh coriander.

Serving suggestions:
Serve with rice or any Indian bread from Chapter 5. Mixed pickle or any raita, plain yoghurt or any fresh chutney will go well with all the vegetarian dishes. It could be an additional dish with the meat curries or with lentils.

2.   Aubergine and potato curry (Baagun Aloo)
Serves: 2-3

Ingredients:
4-6 medium peeled potatoes cut in small chunks
1 aubergine
1 chopped large onion
1 fresh tomato or 1 tablespoon of tomato puree
½ teaspoon of garlic
½ teaspoon of ginger
¼ teaspoon of turmeric
½ teaspoon of red chilli powder or 1 teaspoon of paprika
1 teaspoon of garam masala
1 teaspoon of cumin seeds
Salt to taste
2-3 tablespoons of cooking oil of your choice
Fresh coriander for garnishing

Method:
Heat the cooking oil in a pan and fry the chopped onions until golden-brown. Add the spices, ginger, garlic and the tomato. Stir for 10-20 seconds and then add the potato and aubergine chunks. Stir everything and add ½ cup of water and cook for 2-3 minutes on high heat with the lid on the pan. Then on a medium heat, continue to cook until the vegetables are cooked and all the liquid is dried. Garnish with chopped fresh coriander.

Serving suggestions:
Serve with rice or any Indian bread from Chapter 5. Mixed pickle or any raita, plain yoghurt or any fresh chutney will go well with all the vegetarian dishes. It could be an additional dish with the meat curries or with lentils.

3.   Cauliflower and potato curry (Phool Gobi and Aloo)

Serves 2-3

Ingredients:
4 medium peeled potatoes cut in chunks
2 small or 1 large carrots peeled and diced.
1 medium cauliflower cut into small florets
1 chopped large onion
1 fresh tomato or 1 tablespoon of tomato puree
½ teaspoon of garlic
½ teaspoon of ginger
¼ teaspoon of turmeric
1 teaspoon of cumin seeds
1 teaspoon of garam masala
½ teaspoon of mustard seeds
½ teaspoon of red chilli powder or 1 teaspoon of paprika
Salt to taste
3-4 tablespoons of cooking oil of your choice
Fresh coriander for garnishing

Method:
Heat the cooking oil in a pan and fry the chopped onions until golden-brown. Add the cumin and the mustard seeds. Stir until the seeds start popping and add rest of the spices, ginger, garlic and the tomato. Stir for 10-20 seconds and then add the potato chunks and carrots. Stir to mix everything and add ½ cup of water and cook the potatoes and the diced carrots for 2-3 minutes on high heat; with the lid on the pan. Then add the florets of the cauliflower. Stir to mix and continue to cook on low heat until the vegetables are cooked and all the liquid is dried. Garnish with chopped fresh coriander.

Serving suggestions:
Serve the vegetable curry with rice or any Indian bread from Chapter 5. Mixed pickle or any raita, plain yoghurt or any fresh chutney will go well with all the vegetarian dishes. It could be an additional dish with the meat curries or with lentils

4. Fresh spinach and potato curry (Palak and Aloo)

Serves 2-3

Ingredients:
4-6 medium peeled potatoes cut in small chunks
200g of chopped fresh spinach
1 chopped large onion
1-2 fresh tomatoes or 1 tablespoon of tomato puree
½ teaspoon of garlic
½ teaspoon of ginger
¼ teaspoon of turmeric
¼-½ teaspoon of red chilli powder or 1 teaspoon of paprika
1 teaspoon of sesame seeds
1 teaspoon cumin seeds
1 teaspoon of garam masala
Salt to taste
2-3 tablespoons of cooking oil of your choice

For garnishing: finely chopped onion, small green chilli and tomato, salt to taste and a squeeze of lemon juice.

Method:
Heat the cooking oil in a pan and fry the chopped onions until golden-brown. Add the spices and both the seeds, ginger, garlic and the tomato. Stir for 10-20 seconds and then add the potato chunks. Stir everything and add ½ cup of water and cook the potatoes for 5-6 minutes on high heat; with the lid on the pan. Then add the chopped fresh spinach. Stir to mix and continue to cook on low heat until the vegetables are cooked and all the liquid is dried. Garnish with a finely chopped onion and a small green chilli with a squeeze of lemon.

Serving suggestions:
Serve the vegetable curry with rice or any Indian bread from Chapter 5. Mixed pickle or any raita, plain yoghurt or any fresh chutney will go well with all the vegetarian dishes. It could be an additional dish with the meat curries or with the lentils.

5. Mooli, Palak and Aloo curry (Indian white radish, spinach and potato curry)

Serves 2-3

Ingredients:
3-5 medium peeled potatoes cut in chunks
200g of chopped fresh spinach
1 peeled and diced mooli
1 chopped large onion
1-2 fresh tomatoes or 1 tablespoon of tomato puree
½ teaspoon of garlic
¼ teaspoon of turmeric
¼-½ teaspoon of red chilli powder or 1 teaspoon of paprika
1 teaspoon of cumin seeds
1 teaspoon of garam masala
Salt to taste
3-4 tablespoons of cooking oil of your choice
Fresh coriander for garnishing

Method:
Heat the cooking oil in a pan and fry the chopped onions until golden-brown. Add the spices, garlic and the tomato. Stir for 10-20 seconds and then add the potato chunks and the diced mooli. Stir to mix everything and add ½ cup of water and cook the potatoes and the mooli for 4-5 minutes on high heat; with the lid on the pan. Then add the chopped fresh spinach. Stir to mix and continue to cook on low heat until the vegetables are cooked and all the liquid is dried. Garnish with a finely chopped onion and a small green chilli with a squeeze of lemon.

Serving suggestions:
Serve the vegetable curry with rice or any Indian bread from Chapter 5. Mixed pickle or any raita, plain yoghurt or any fresh chutney will go well with all the vegetarian dishes. It could be an additional dish with the meat curries or with lentils.

6.   Courgettes, red pepper and potato curry

Serves 2-3

Ingredients:
3-5 medium peeled potatoes cut in small chunks
1 red pepper cut into chunks
2 courgettes cut into small slices or chunks
2 chopped large onions
1 fresh tomato or 1 tablespoon of tomato puree
½ teaspoon of garlic
¼ teaspoon of ginger
¼ teaspoon of turmeric
¼-½ teaspoon of red chilli powder or 1 teaspoon of paprika
1 teaspoon of garam masala
Salt to taste
3-4 tablespoons of cooking oil of your choice
Fresh coriander for garnishing

Method:
Heat the cooking oil in a pan and fry the chopped onions until golden-brown. Add the spices, ginger, garlic and the tomato. Stir for 10-20 seconds and then add the potato chunks. Stir to mix everything and add ½ cup of water and cook the potatoes for 2-3 minutes on high heat; with the lid on the pan. Then add the red pepper and the courgettes. Stir to mix and continue to cook on low heat until the vegetables are cooked and all the liquid is dried. Garnish with chopped fresh coriander or water cress or chives.

Serving suggestions:
Serve the vegetable curry with rice or any Indian bread from Chapter 5. Mixed pickle or any raita, plain yoghurt or any fresh chutney will go well with all the vegetarian dishes. It could be an additional dish with the meat curries or with lentils.

7. Cabbage, carrots and potatoes curry (bundh Gobi, gaajer and aloo)

Serves 2-3

Ingredients:
1 small white cabbage
1 medium carrot
2-3 medium potatoes
2 large onions
1 fresh tomato or 1 tablespoon of tomato puree
½ teaspoon of garlic
½ teaspoon of ginger
¼ teaspoon of turmeric
¼-½ teaspoon of red chilli powder or 1 teaspoon of paprika
1 teaspoon of whole mustard seeds (optional)
1 teaspoon of cumin seeds
Salt to taste
2-3 tablespoons of cooking oil of your choice
Fresh coriander for garnishing

Method:
Shred the cabbage and the carrots in a food processor. Peel and cut the potatoes into cubes or fairly small pieces. Heat the cooking oil in a pan and fry the chopped onions until golden-brown. Add the spices, ginger, garlic and tomato. Stir for 5-6 seconds and then add the potato cubes and the shredded cabbage and carrots. Stir and add ½ cup of water; cover the pan with the lid. Continue to cook all the vegetables on medium heat. Take the pan off the heat when vegetables are cooked and all the liquid has dried. Transfer the curry into the serving dish and garnish with chopped fresh coriander or water cress or chives.

Serving suggestions:
Serve the vegetable curry with rice or any Indian bread from Chapter 5. It could also be an additional dish with the meat curries or with lentils.

8.   Bhandi (Okra) and onions curry

Serves 1-2

Ingredients:
50-100g of fresh or frozen chopped bhandi
1-2 large chopped onions
2 fresh tomato or 1 tablespoon of tomato puree
1 chopped green chilli
¼ teaspoon of turmeric
½ teaspoon of paprika
Salt to taste
2-3 tablespoons of cooking oil of your choice
Fresh coriander for garnishing

Method:
Heat the cooking oil in a pan and fry the chopped onions for 30 seconds and then add the chopped okra. Keep frying for another 2 minutes and then add the tomatoes and rest of the spices. Stir and add a splash of water on the vegetables. Cover the pan and leave it on low heat until the okra is cooked. Garnish with chopped fresh coriander or water cress or chives.

Serving suggestions:
Serve the bhandi curry with rice or any Indian bread from Chapter 5. It could also be an additional dish with the meat curries or with the lentils.

9.   Eggs and potato curry (Aunday Aloo)

Serves 3-4

Ingredients:
4-6 boiled and shelled eggs
5-6 medium sized peeled potatoes cut in chunks
Fresh chopped coriander for garnishing

Method:
Use recipe A from Chapter 3 to prepare the curry sauce and to the half of the basic curry sauce add the chunks of the potatoes and 1-2 cups of water (refrigerate or freeze the other half of the curry sauce for some other curry).

Cover the pan with the lid and cook the potatoes on medium heat. When the potatoes are almost cooked add the boiled and shelled eggs and simmer the curry until the potatoes are completely cooked. The consistency of the sauce should be fairly thick. Take it off the heat and garnish with chopped fresh coriander or water cress or chives.

Serving suggestions:
Serve with rice or any Indian bread from Chapter 5. Mixed pickle or any fresh chutney will go well with all the vegetarian dishes.

10. Indian egg omelette

Serves 1-2

Ingredients:
2-4 large whisked eggs
2 finely chopped small spring onions or 1 medium finely chopped onion
1 small finely chopped green chilli
1 tablespoon of chopped green coriander or parsley or spinach
1 medium chopped tomato
Handful of diced red and green pepper
Turmeric, just the tip of a teaspoon
¼ teaspoon ground or whole cumin seeds
¼ teaspoon of black pepper
2 tablespoons of butter or cooking oil
Salt to taste

Method:
Add butter/oil to a frying pan and soften the onion on medium heat. Then add the pepper, the tomato and all the other ingredients, except the eggs and stir until all the liquid from the tomato has dried. *Now add the whisked eggs, stir gently until the egg starts to thicken. Lift up the cooked part of the egg by using a fork and allow the uncooked and runny portion of the egg to run underneath the cooked egg. Continue to cook until the egg is firm. Using a flat spatula turn the omelette over to cook the topside of the omelette for another 10-20 seconds.

* (Alternative method) Now add the whisked eggs, stir gently until the egg starts to thicken and continue to stir and cook the egg like you make scrambled egg.

Serving suggestions:
Serve with any Indian bread from Chapter 5 or any other bread. Plain paratha with omelette and pickle is very common and popular combination among the Pakistani/Indians.

11. Lentils and beans (daals)

Daals are rich in proteins and are a good vegetarian alternative to meat. Daals are also rich in carbohydrates, mineral and vitamins and are virtually fat-free. The common daals used by Indians are red lentils (Lal Masoor daal), green lentils, Moong daal (Mung beans), Chana daal (split chickpeas), Lowbiya (black eye beans), and Urid daal. These daals are available as whole or spilt. Unlike the beans the lentils don't require overnight soaking but 1-2 hours soaking is suffice. Most of the daals are cooked the same way; the only difference is that some take little longer to cook than the others.

Note to remember:
When buying the daals, check the expiry date and see if the lentils look healthy in colour and not shrivelled or dried up.

Before cooking, make sure you always wash the daal in a sieve, under running tap water. This should get rid of all the dust and the grit, if there was any present.

A squeeze of lemon and plain yoghurt enhances the taste of all cooked lentils and beans.

11a. Red lentils daal (all daals are cooked using this recipe)

Serves 3-4

Ingredients:
200-250g of red split lentil ((Masoor daal)
1 medium chopped onion
1 fresh finely chopped tomato or 1 tablespoon of tomato puree

1 small chopped green chilli
1 teaspoon of cumin seeds
1 teaspoon of garlic (fresh or puree)
1 teaspoon of fresh grated ginger or powder ginger
½-1 teaspoon of turmeric
½-1 teaspoon of red chilli powder
1 teaspoon of garam masala
1 teaspoon of whole mustard seeds is optional
Salt to taste
2-3 tablespoons of cooking oil of your choice
Fresh coriander for garnishing

Method:
In a suitable saucepan put the washed red lentils and enough water to cover the daal. Put it over high heat and boil for 2-3 minutes. At this stage all daals get very frothy and can produce a scum. Using a cooking spoon or a ladle, try to remove the scum and discard it. Then reduce the heat and add the turmeric, red chilli powder, garam masala, garlic and ginger with a sprinkle of salt. (The addition of few chunks of potatoes and carrots to the daal makes the dish wholesome). Cook until the daal is cooked and is creamy in texture. Add more salt to your taste. In a hot frying pan put some cooking oil and fry the chopped onions until golden-brown. Reduce the heat and add the cumin seeds, whole mustard seeds, the tomatoes and the green chopped chilli. Stir for few seconds and then pour it over the cooked lentils. Garnish with chopped fresh coriander or water cress or chives.

Serving suggestions:
Serve with rice or any Indian bread from Chapter 5. Mixed pickle or cucumber/boodni raita, salsa, plain yoghurt or any fresh chutney will go well with all the lentil dishes.

11b. Black Eye Beans or red kidney beans (Lowbiya) curry

Serves 3-4

Ingredients:
200-250g of the beans of your choice
2 large chopped onions
½-1 tin of tomatoes or 2-3 tablespoons of tomato puree

1 small chopped green chilli
1 teaspoon of cumin seeds
1 teaspoon of garlic (fresh or puree)
1 teaspoon of fresh grated ginger or powder ginger
½ teaspoon of turmeric
½ teaspoon of red chilli powder
1 teaspoon of garam masala
Salt to taste
2-3 tablespoons of cooking oil of your choice
Fresh coriander for garnishing

Method:
Like the daals, beans need to be washed before soaking and cooking. Soak the beans for at least 3-4 hours. Soaking overnight will reduce the cooking time. In a suitable saucepan put some cooking oil and on the medium heat fry the onions until slightly brown. Reduce the heat and add the cumin seed and stir for a couple of seconds. Add the rest of the ingredients. Stir for another minute and then add the washed and the soaked beans. Add about 2-3 cups of water and cook on medium heat until the beans are well cooked. Don't forget to add salt and keep the sauce of the cooked beans fairly thick. Garnish with chopped fresh coriander or water cress or chives.

Serving suggestions:
Serve with rice or any Indian bread from Chapter 5. Mixed pickle or any raita, salsa, plain yoghurt or any fresh chutney goes well with the dish.

12. Lentils and the vegetable curry
Fresh chopped palak (spinach) and chana daal (most of the vegetables work well with all the daals)

Serves 3-4

Ingredients:
Fresh chopped spinach 200g
200g of washed and soaked (1-2 hours) daal
1 medium chopped onion
1 fresh finely chopped tomato or 1 tablespoon of tomato puree or ½ tin of tomato
1 small chopped green chilli

1 teaspoon of cumin seeds
½ teaspoon of garlic (fresh or puree)
1 teaspoon of fresh grated ginger or powder ginger
½ teaspoon of turmeric
½ teaspoon of red chilli powder
1 teaspoon of garam masala
1 teaspoon of whole mustard seeds
Salt to taste
2-3 tablespoons of cooking oil of your choice

Method:
Heat the oil in a suitable pan and fry the chopped onion. Add all the spices to the frying onions and then add a cup of water and the daal and cook on high heat. Take care that the daal is cooked but does not go mushy. To the cooked daal add the finely chopped spinach and simmer until the spinach is cooked and the all the liquid is dried.

Serving suggestions:
Serve spinach and chana daal curry with rice or any Indian bread from Chapter 5. Mixed pickle or any raita, salsa, plain yoghurt or any fresh chutney goes well with the dish.

13. Pakoras Curry (baysen karhee)

Serves 3-4

The curry sauce of this dish is very different from all the other curries. It is yellow in colour, and the consistency is similar to yoghurt/custard and it is spicy and tangy in taste.

Prepare the pakoras using recipe No: 19 of Chapter 2

Preparation of the Sauce:

Ingredients:
4 tablespoons of baysen (chickpea flour)
¾ cup of dahi (homemade yoghurt, see recipe No: 24 of Chapter 2)
1 medium chopped onion
½ teaspoon of chilli powder

½ teaspoon of turmeric
1 tablespoon of ground coriander
1 teaspoon of garam masala
¼ teaspoon of fenugreek (seeds or powder)
1 teaspoon of mustard seeds
1 teaspoon of crushed garlic
1 teaspoon of crushed ginger
Salt to taste
2 tablespoons of cooking oil
Handful of fresh coriander for garnishing

Method:
In a suitable bowl thoroughly mix yoghurt and baysen (chickpea flour), ensuring there are no lumps. Add 2 cups of water gradually and give a good mix and leave it aside.

Fry the chopped onions in a suitable saucepan, put the cumin seeds and fenugreek seeds in the pan, toast for 1-2 seconds; then add rest of the ingredients. Stir for a minute and then pour all the yoghurt mixture. Bring to the boil and then simmer on low heat for 15-20 minutes. Stir the mixture from time to time as the mixture starts thickening. Add 8-10 vegetable pakoras and simmer for another 4-5 minutes. The consistency of the sauce should be like runny custard. Take it off the heat and garnish with the fresh chopped coriander or water cress or chives.

Serving suggestions:
Normally this dish is eaten with boiled rice but it also goes well with naan bread/chapati.

14. Vegetable Korma

The vegetable Korma is also called Nauo Rattan (nine gems) because the dish is made with nine different vegetables and thus makes it a special and a prestigious vegetarian dish. *Please see all the notes for recipe: No. 11 for the meat/vegetable korma in Chapter 3B.*

Vegetable korma:

Serves 3-4

Ingredients:
300-400g of washed and chopped carrots, cauliflower, potatoes, green beans, courgettes, peas, aubergines, butter beans and sweet corn (add or eliminate any vegetables you prefer)
50-100g cubes of homemade paneer is optional
Handful of nuts/ seeds of your choice (cashew nuts are the popular ones but pumpkin/sesame seeds can be used)
2 large chopped onions
1 tablespoon of garam masala
1 tablespoon of ground coriander
¼ teaspoon of turmeric
½-1 teaspoon of red chillies
2 teaspoons of desiccated coconut or 2 tablespoons of coconut milk (optional)
1 tablespoon of ground poppy seeds or 1 tablespoon of ground almonds
½ cup of plain yoghurt
1 small chopped green chilli
Fresh chopped ginger, about 1 tablespoon
1 teaspoon crushed garlic
Salt to taste
A handful of fresh coriander for garnishing
Cooking oil

Note to remember: Please don't forget to eliminate any intolerant ingredients.

Method:
In a suitable bowl put all the ingredients except the yoghurt and the chopped onions. Mix it well so that all the vegetables and paneer, nuts/ seeds are well coated with the spices. Marinate it for at least for an hour. Fry the chopped onions in 3-4 tablespoons of oil in a suitable saucepan until light brown. Reduce the heat and add the marinated mixture and keep stirring on a medium heat for 3-4 minutes. Take the pan off the heat and let it cool before adding the yoghurt as at a high temperature the yoghurt will separate from its liquid. When it is slightly cooler (from hot to warm) add half of the yoghurt and mix it with the vegetables.

Mix it thoroughly and put it back on a medium heat, and cover the pan with the lid. Continue cooking for 2-3 minutes. Take the pan off the heat and let it cool (from hot to warm) before adding rest of the yoghurt. Add the remaining yoghurt, mixing it thoroughly and put it back on the medium heat, covering the pan with the lid until the vegetables are cooked and the remaining sauce is very thick but moist. (Add some water if the vegetables run dry). Garnish with fresh coriander or water cress or chives.

Serving suggestions:
Serve with rice or any Indian bread from Chapter 5. Mixed pickle or any fresh chutney will enhance the taste.

Chapter 4

Rice

The aromatic variety of long and thin rice of India/Pakistan is basmati, traditionally used in the pulaos and the biryani dishes. The maturity of the rice improves the flavour and cooks better than rice of the new crop. The washing of rice before cooking removes any starch sticking on the rice and this prevents the grains of rice sticking to each other. The soaking of rice helps the grains to swell and to increase to its maximum length, and also helps the rice to withstand long cooking without breaking. Most of the rice expands twice its size, when cooked. The rice is cooked on fairly high heat to begin with and simmered when the middle of the rice grain remains uncooked or when two-thirds of the rice grain is cooked.

☺ *A good simmering technique is to cover the rice first with the kitchen foil or a damp tea towel and then to cover the pan with the lid.*

Note to remember:

❖ ® *How to work out the required volume of water:*
❖ *The workable ratio of **rice: water is 1:2**, when you are making the pulao dishes. It is helpful to put the weighed rice in the measuring jug and measure the volume of rice in millilitres (ml).* ® *The required volume of water is almost double the volume of rice and some extra water is added for cooking the meat or the vegetable, or use 1 cup/mug of rice and 2 cups/mugs of water.*
❖ *In case you have added too much water in making the pulao rice, then take off the lid and carefully evaporate the excess liquid on a fairly high heat, without burning the rice at the bottom of the pan.*

❖ *In case you haven't added enough water while making the pulao rice, then add splashes of hot water, put the lid back on the pan and continue to simmer the rice.*

❖ *When dishing out the rice, don't forget to take out the whole spices.*

Note to remember: *Please go through the recipes cautiously to check if you are sensitive or intolerant to any of the ingredients and make sure to eliminate or to use a suitable alternative.*

The Rice Dishes:

1.   Boiled Rice or Plain rice

Serves 1-2

Ingredients:
70-140g (roughly 2-4 handfuls) basmati rice
Seeds of 1-2 green cardamoms
2-3 whole black cloves
½ ⁱⁿᶜʰ of cinnamon stick
1 tablespoon of cooking oil (prevents rice sticking)
Salt to taste

Method:
Wash the rice in the sieve under running tap water. Soak the washed rice in warm water for at least 30 minutes. In a suitable saucepan pour plenty of water (as you do when boiling pasta and spaghetti). Put rest of the ingredients in and bring to the boil. Boil for at least 4-5 minutes to give time for the cloves, cinnamon and the cardamom to release their flavours. Drain the water from the soaking rice and add the rice to the boiling water. Boil the rice for 5-6 minutes on a fairly high heat. Take it off the heat and strain the boiled rice in a colander and then transfer the rice back to the saucepan. Put the lid on the pan and let the rice simmer on very low heat; until the rice is cooked and fluffy.

Alternatively you can make plain rice by using the above recipe but use the right volume of water (see notes ® *How to work out the required volume of water*) to cook the rice on fairly heat until all the water is absorbed.

Turn the heat down and simmer the rice on very low heat; until the rice is cooked and fluffy. ☺ *See the note on simmering techniques.*

Serving suggestions:
Plain boiled rice goes well with all of the lentil, vegetable and meat curries. Try the boiled rice with chicken tikka, with the different kinds of kebabs and with tandoori chicken. In addition select what you prefer from Chapter 6, the choice of the condiments, chutneys, raitas and different kinds of pickles.

What is Pulao rice?

A pulao is when the rice is cooked in a meat or fish or vegetable broth flavoured with brown onions and with several different spices.

2.   Mutter pulao rice (Peas pulao rice)

Chickpea or mixed vegetable can also be used to make this pulao rice

Serves 1-2

Ingredients:
70-140g (roughly 2-4 handfuls) basmati rice
½-1 cup of frozen peas or ½-1 tin of chickpeas
See notes ® How to work out the required volume of water
2 ^{inches} of cinnamon stick
1-2 black cardamoms
Seeds of one green cardamom
2-3 whole black cloves
1 teaspoon of cumin seeds
1-2 bay leaves
2 tablespoons of cooking oil
Salt to taste

Method:
Wash and soak the rice in warm water. In a suitable saucepan put some cooking oil and on medium heat fry the onions golden-brown. Reduce the heat and add all the spices. Stir for 2-3 seconds and then put the peas or chickpeas in and stir for another minute. Add the right volume of water and cover the pan with the lid (see notes® *How to work out the required volume of water*). Bring to the boil

and let it boil for 4-5 minutes for the onions to give their colour and flavour. This will also give time for the cloves, cumin and cardamom to release their aromas and for the peas to cook. Drain the water from the soaking rice and add the rice to the pan, stir to mix and put the lid back on the pan. Continue to cook and do not stir the rice too much but make sure that there is enough water for the rice to swell and to cook. When most of the liquid is absorbed by the rice and only the middle of the rice grain remains uncooked then let the rice simmer on a very low heat; until the rice is cooked and fluffy. ☺ *See the note on simmering techniques.* If the rice is not cooked after simmering then add a splash of hot water and continue to simmer until completely cooked.

Serving suggestions:
Mutter (peas) pulao rice goes well with all the vegetable and meat curries. Try the pulao with the chicken tikka or with the different kinds of kebabs or with tandoori chicken. In addition select what you prefer from Chapter 6, the choice of condiments, chutneys, raitas and different kinds of pickles.

3.   Goshtt pulao rice (Meat pulao rice)

Lamb, beef, chicken or any meat can be used for making meat pulao rice

Serves 3-4

Ingredients:
5-8 skinned chicken drum sticks or thighs
200-300g reasonably sized pieces of lamb (if making lamb pulao)
210-280g (roughly 6-8 handfuls) basmati rice—washed and soaked in warm water
See notes ® *How to work out the required volume of water)* but add extra 100/150ml for the meat
2 ^{inches} of cinnamon stick
Seeds of 2 green cardamoms
2 whole black cardamoms
3-4 whole black cloves
4-5 black peppercorns
2 teaspoons of cumin seeds
1-2 bay leaves
2-3 tablespoons of cooking oil
1 teaspoon of grated ginger

3 cloves of garlic
Salt to taste
1 medium chopped onion

Method:
In a suitable saucepan put some cooking oil, and on medium heat fry the onions golden-brown. Add all the spices and fry them for 20 seconds, then add the meat and keep on stirring until the meat is brown. Add the water and cover the pan with the lid and cook until the meat is nearly cooked. Drain the water from the rice and then add the rice to the pan with the meat. Mix the meat and the rice. Put the lid back and carry on cooking until all the liquid is absorbed and the rice and meat is almost cooked. Simmer the rice on the low heat; until the rice is cooked and fluffy

☺ *See the note on simmering techniques.*

Serving suggestions:
All yoghurt raitas, green chutneys and pickles go well with the meat pulao rice. All curries with runny sauce are popular with the pulao.

4.   Keema Chawal (Mincemeat and rice)

Serves 3-4

Ingredients:
1 large chopped onion
250-300g beef mince (chicken or lamb or turkey mince is as good as the beef mince or quorn for vegetarians)
1 finely chopped carrot
1 tablespoon of ground coriander
1 teaspoon of garam masala
½ teaspoon of turmeric
1 teaspoon of chilli powder
1 teaspoon of garlic (fresh and crushed)
1 teaspoon of ginger (fresh and crushed)
1 tin of tomatoes
1-2 tins of red beans (washed with water)
210-280g (roughly 6-8 handfuls) basmati rice (washed and soaked)
Chopped fresh coriander for garnishing

Method:
In a suitable saucepan put some cooking oil and on the medium heat fry the onions until golden-brown. Add the chopped carrots, all the spices and fry them for 30-40 seconds and then add the mincemeat and keep on stirring until the meat is nicely brown. Then add a tin of tomatoes and red beans. Mix them well with the meat and then add a cup of water and continue to cook until the meat and the beans are cooked. Garnish with chopped green coriander and serve with the boiled rice.

Boil the rice using recipe No: 1of Chapter 4.

Serving suggestions:
Salad leaves or onion and tomato salsa or green yoghurt chutney or lime pickle will enhance the taste of the dish.

5. Meat biryani

Chicken, lamb, beef or any meat can be used for making meat biryani.

Serves 3-4

Ingredients:
200-300g of diced boneless meat
210-280g (roughly 6-8 handfuls) basmati rice—washed and soaked in warm water
¾ cup of plain yoghurt
1 tablespoons of ground coriander
1teaspoon of garam masala
½ teaspoon of turmeric
½ teaspoon of chilli powder
1 small green chopped chilli
1 large chopped onion
Garlic and ginger to taste
2 large chopped fresh tomatoes or tinned tomatoes or tomato puree can be used
2 medium potatoes sliced and boiled in salted water for 2-3 minutes and drained
3-4 tablespoons of cooking oil

Method:
In a suitable bowl add the yoghurt, all the spices (and that includes the ginger and garlic, the green chilli and the salt). Mix thoroughly. Add the diced meat and coat with the spiced yoghurt by stirring and leave it to marinate at least for 1-2 hours or more.

Boil the rice using the recipe No: 1 of Chapter 4; leave the cooked rice ready for the further step.

Put some cooking oil in a saucepan and on the medium heat fry the onions until golden-brown. Add the chopped tomatoes and cook for 1-2 minutes. Add the meat with all the marinade and keep stirring and cook it on a medium heat for 3-4 minutes. Cover the pan with a lid and let it simmer on a very low heat until the meat is cooked. The meat and the potato slices are ready for making the alternative layers with boiled rice in a saucepan or using an oven dish.

Take the oven dish lined with butter. Start with a layer of boiled rice, then a layer of cooked meat and some partially cooked potatoes. Repeat the layer of rice then a layer of meat and potatoes until you have used all the cooked ingredients. Make sure that the first and the top layer is with the rice. Cover the dish with kitchen foil and place the dish in the preheated oven at 180^0C/355^0F/Gas 4 for 15-20 minutes.

If using a saucepan, butter the bottom of the pan. Start with a layer of boiled rice, then a layer of cooked meat and some partially cooked potatoes. Repeat the layers of rice then of the meat and potatoes until you have used all the cooked ingredients. Make sure that you end the top layer with the rice. Add 1 or 2 splashes of water and simmer on a very low heat for 10-15 minutes. ☺ *See the note on simmering techniques.*

Garnish with chopped coriander, very thinly sliced lemon and fried onions. Spread a handful of sultanas and roasted almonds for further garnishing.

Serving suggestions:
All yoghurt sauces (raitas), all green chutneys and all pickles go well with the meat biryani.

6. Vegetable biryani

Serves 3-4

Ingredients:
200-300g of mixed vegetables (carrots, peas, sweet corn, green beans)
210-280g (roughly 6-8 handfuls) basmati rice—washed and soaked in warm water
¾ cup of plain yoghurt
2 tablespoons of ground coriander
1 teaspoon of garam masala
½ teaspoon of turmeric
¼ teaspoon of chilli powder
1 small green chopped chilli
1 large chopped onion
Garlic and ginger to taste
2 large chopped fresh tomatoes or tin tomatoes/tomato puree can be used
2 medium potatoes sliced and boiled in salted water for 2 minutes and drained
2-3 tablespoons of cooking oil

Method:
In a suitable bowl add the yoghurt, all the spices (and that includes the ginger and garlic, the green chilli and the salt). Mix thoroughly. Add the mixed vegetables and coat with the spiced yoghurt by stirring and leave to marinate at least for 1-2 hours.

Boil the rice using the recipe No: 1 of Chapter 4; leave the cooked rice ready for the further step.

Put some cooking oil in a saucepan and on the medium heat fry the onions until golden-brown. Add the chopped tomatoes and cook for 1-2 minutes. Then add the vegetables with all the marinade and keep stirring and cook on a medium heat for 3-4 minutes. Cover the pan with a lid and let it simmer on a very low heat until the vegetables are almost cooked. The vegetable and the potato slices are ready for creating the alternative layers with the boiled rice in a saucepan or using an oven dish.

Take the oven dish lined with butter. Start with a layer of boiled rice, then a layer of cooked vegetables and some partially cooked potatoes. Repeat the layers of rice then of the vegetables and potatoes until you have used all the cooked ingredients. Make sure that the first and the top layers are rice. Cover the dish with kitchen foil and place the dish in the preheated oven at180°C/355° F/Gas 4 for 10-15 minutes.

If using a saucepan, butter the bottom of the pan. Start with a layer of boiled rice, then a layer of cooked vegetables and some partially cooked potatoes. Repeat the layers of rice then of the vegetables and then of potatoes until you have used all the cooked ingredients. Make sure that you finish with a layer of rice. Simmer on a very low heat for 10-15 minutes. ☺ *See the note on simmering techniques.*

Garnish with chopped coriander, very thinly sliced lemon and fried onions. Spread a handful of sultanas, cashew nuts and roasted almonds for further garnishing.

Serving suggestions:
All yoghurt sauces (raitas), green chutneys and pickles go well with the meat biryani.

7. Fish biryani (with peas and potatoes)

Serves: 2-3

Ingredients:
Marinate 4-6 pieces of fish lightly with salt and pepper and a little lemon juice, for 20-30 minutes and shallow fry the fish for a minute each side.
140-210g (roughly 4-6 handfuls) basmati rice—washed and soaked in warm water
2 tablespoons of ground coriander
1 teaspoon of ground cumin/cumin seeds
1 teaspoon of garam masala
½ teaspoon of turmeric
½ teaspoon of chilli powder
1 small green chopped chilli
1 large chopped onion
Garlic and ginger to taste

2 large chopped fresh tomatoes or half a tin of tomatoes or tomato puree can be used

3-4 medium potatoes sliced and 100g of peas; both boiled in salted water for 3-4 minutes and drained.

2-3 tablespoons of cooking oil

Method:

Boil the rice using the recipe No: 1 of Chapter 4; leave the cooked rice ready for the further step.

In a suitable saucepan put some cooking oil and on the medium heat fry the onions until golden-brown. Add garlic, ginger and the chopped tomatoes. Then add all the other spices and stir everything with 50ml of water. Place the lid and continue to cook. When the liquid dries up, take the pan from the heat and add the fried fish, the peas and the potatoes to the sauce. Mix everything together without breaking the potatoes and the fish pieces and simmer for 1-2 minutes. The fish mixture is ready for making the alternative layers with the boiled rice in a saucepan or using an oven dish.

Take the oven dish lined with butter. Start with a layer of boiled rice, then a layer of the fish mixture. Repeat the layer of rice then of the fish mixture until you have used all the ingredients. Make sure that the first and the top layer is rice. Cover the dish with kitchen foil and place the dish in the preheated oven at180 ^{0}C/355^0 F/Gas 4 for 10-15 minutes.

If using a saucepan, butter the bottom of the pan. Start with a layer of boiled rice, then a layer of the fish mixture. Repeat the layer of rice then the fish mixture until you have used all the ingredients. Make sure that you end the top layer with rice. Simmer on a very low heat for 10-15 minutes. ☺ *See the note on simmering techniques.*

Garnish with chopped coriander, very thinly sliced lemon and fried onion.

Serving suggestions:

All green chutneys and all pickles go well with the fish biryani.

8. Tahari rice (meat or vegetable curry rice)

Serves 3-4

Tahari is a type of biryani, when rice and meat/vegetable curry is cooked together

Ingredients:
200-300g lamb shoulder/leg chopped into reasonably sized pieces.
2 medium sliced potatoes (use potatoes that will not go mushy)
210-280g (roughly 6-8 handfuls) basmati rice, washed and soaked

See notes ® *How to work out the required volume of water)* and add extra 100-150 ml for the meat and the vegetable

Method:
Prepare the basic curry sauce using only one medium onion and only one tablespoon of tomato puree or ¼ tin of tomatoes using the curry sauce recipe A of Chapter 3. Wash the meat in a colander, drain the water and stir the meat into the curry sauce. Put the pan on a medium heat and cook the meat for 2-3 minutes. Pour the right volume of water and continue to cook until the meat is almost cooked. Then add the sliced potatoes and the rice. Cook until all the liquid is absorbed and then simmer on low heat until the meat, the potatoes and the rice are cooked. ☺ *See the simmering techniques.*

Serving suggestions:
All yoghurt raitas, all green chutneys and all pickles go well with tahari rice.

9. Khichri (Kedgeree)

The Punjabi khichri is rice and any daal cooked together into creamy rice with either no fat or very small amount of fat. This is normally served with some plain yoghurt. Moong daal is gentle to the stomach and well-cooked khichri is easy to digest. But the same dish of rice and the chana daal is cooked like the pulao rice with fat and basmati rice. But for the creamy khichri the broken rice or small round rice can be used. These two khichries are the popular ones but one can use the other lentils and the beans using the same recipes.

Unlike the English Kedgeree, neither fish nor boiled egg is used in the Punjabi khichri and it is not particularly made for the breakfast though khichri can be eaten for that meal if preferred.

9A. The Khichri for the tender stomach
Traditionally this is the diet used for the unwell, for the elderly and even a solid food for the babies too.

Serves 1-2

Ingredients:
60-120g of broken or small round rice
20-50g skinned and split moong daal (washed and soaked for 2-3 hours)
2 ^{inches} of cinnamon stick
Seeds of one green cardamom
2 black cardamoms
2-3 whole black cloves
1 teaspoon of ground cumin
Salt to taste

See notes ® *How to work out the required volume of water*, add 100-150 ml for cooking the daal

Method:
Wash and soak the rice in warm water (soaked for 1-2 hours). In a suitable saucepan put all the whole spices with the right volume of water and bring to boil for 4-5 minutes. Drain the water from the soaking rice and the daal and add to the pan. Stir to mix and put the lid back on the pan. Stir from time to time; making sure that there is enough water for the rice and the daal to swell and to cook. In this case we are not worried about keeping the rice grain separate because the aim is to make creamy rice. This is something which could be suitable to a tender stomach.

Serving suggestions:
Serve with plain yoghurt.

9B. Chana daal Khichri

Serves 1-2

Ingredients:
60-120g of basmati rice
30-60g of chana daal washed and soaked in warm water for 2-3 hours
2 inches of cinnamon stick
Seeds of one green cardamom
2 black cardamoms
2-3 whole black cloves
1 teaspoon of cumin seeds
2-3 tablespoons of butter or cooking oil
Salt to taste

See notes ® *How to work out the required volume of water* and 100ml for cooking the chana daal

Method:
Wash and soak the rice in warm water for 30 minutes. In a suitable saucepan put some cooking oil and on medium heat fry the onions until golden-brown. Reduce the heat and add the cumin seed, the cinnamon, cloves, the seed of the green cardamom stick and the Chana daal, then stir for 20 seconds. Add the right volume of water, and cover the pan with the lid. Bring it to the boil for 3-4 minutes. This will give time for the cloves, cumin and the cardamom to release their flavours and for the daal to cook. Reduce the heat and cook until the Chana daal is almost cooked then drain the water from the soaking rice and add to the pan. Stir to mix and put the lid back on. Cook on a high heat until all the liquid is absorbed, stirring from time to time to ensure there is enough water for the rice to swell and to cook. Then simmer the rice and the daal on a very low heat until the rice and the Chana daal is cooked. ☺ *See the note on simmering techniques.*

Note to remember: If the rice/daal are not cooked after simmering; add a splash of warm water and continue to simmer until the rice and daal are completely cooked. If you have added too much water, then take off the lid and carefully evaporate the excess of liquid whilst on a high heat.

Serving suggestions:

Chana daal Khichri is served with green chutneys or just plain yoghurt or yoghurt with the fresh chutney and with all types of pickles. It goes well with the meat curries, with chicken tikka, different kinds of kebabs and tandoori chicken.

Chapter 5

Indian Breads

Wheat is a grain which grows all over the world and is commonly used for making bread. It's naturally rich in a protein which has the capacity to absorb water quickly and develops a sticky protein called gluten. This gluten gives the elasticity to the dough and holds the dough together in any shape. It is not enough to simply make the dough; kneading is essential. The kneading is important because during this process the dough is stretched, pulled and pressed. This makes the strands of the gluten long, tough and flexible. This makes it possible to roll and to pat the dough into any shape and to make it as thin as required and also gives a good soft texture to the bread. When cooked, these gluten strands are solidified or coagulate just as protein in an egg is cooked. The Indian breads made from the wheat flour are chapati, paratha, naan, poori and prooray. Whereas baysen ki roti and dosa are the gluten-free breads made with the flour of the chana daal, rice and the urid daal.

Note to remember: Please go through the recipes cautiously to check if you are sensitive or intolerant to any of the ingredients and make sure to eliminate or to use a suitable alternative.

1. Plain Chapati (Roti)

Serves 1-2

A rough and quick measurement of flour to make one chapati is 1 handful, and to be precise, 25g to make one good size chapati.

Ingredients:
50-100g wholemeal chapati flour
¼-½ cup of water for making the dough

Method:
Chapati dough can be made with the old traditional method of using your hands. Place the flour into a suitable bowl with a flat-base metal dish (paraat) and make a well in the centre. Pour some water and start mixing the flour with your fingers. Then with both hands, gradually mix all the flour using splashes of water. Kneading is very important in making Indian breads as it makes the dough strong, smooth and pliable, and above all makes the bread soft. Knead the dough by pushing it away from you with the heel of your hand. Repeat it, working your way through the whole dough. Gather the dough back into a ball and continue kneading for 4-5 minutes. During the kneading if the dough is too sticky then add little more dry flour. Likewise, if the dough is too hard, use splashes of water as you continue kneading until the dough is smooth, soft and elastic.

However, it is an easy and convenient alternative to make the chapati dough in a food processor or in a dough mixer. Put the flour in a food processor and ¼ cup of water to start with and then keep adding splashes of water until the dough forms a soft and smooth ball. Take out the dough and knead it with your hands for 3-5 minutes then cover it with cling film. Leave it in the fridge to rest. While the dough is resting, put a flat pan or a tawa on medium heat. If you prefer to be consistent with the size of the chapati, divide the dough into equal portions. Take one portion and roll it into a ball between the palms of your hands. On the kitchen work surface sprinkle dry flour and **roll the dough as thin as tortilla wraps** by using a rolling pin. After every 2-3 strokes with the rolling pin, lift the dough and sprinkle a bit more dry flour on the work surface. Continue to roll the dough until you get the required thickness and the round shape of a chapati.

Place the rolled chapati on a hot flat pan or a tawa. You will notice that the colour of the uncooked dough changes and small bubbles appear. At this point you need to turn the chapati over using a flat spatula and keep moving it around by using the tongs or spatula to avoid it burning. At this stage if you also press the edges of the chapati, using a flat spatula, it will rise or inflate (like a balloon) and makes its texture light. If you notice that any part of the chapati is uncooked, continue to cook and press the uncooked part down with the flat spatula. You need to cook each side for approximately 30 seconds. Freshly cooked chapati (roti) tastes delicious when you spread a little butter.

Serving suggestions:
Chapatis are normally eaten with curries and lentils. But they can also make good kebab rolls with salads, and egg rolls, and with butter and jam it makes a good jam-roll.

2.   Paratha (plain or stuffed): Paratha is a crispy and a flaky fried chapati.

Plain paratha:

Serves 1-2

Ingredients:
50-100g wholemeal chapati flour
¼-½ cup of water for making the dough
Butter or cooking oil of your choice

Method:
To make dough using your hands see recipe No: 1 of Chapter 5. While the dough is resting, place a flat pan or a tawa on a medium hot hob.

If you prefer to be consistent with the size of the paratha, divide the dough into equal portions. Take one portion and roll it into a ball between the palms of your hands. On the kitchen work surface sprinkle dry flour and roll the dough as thin as tortillas wraps. Brush some butter or cooking oil on it and fold the left and the right side towards the centre, spread more butter/oil on the folds and then fold the top and the bottom side towards the centre. This square shaped dough with butter/oil is rolled slightly thicker than a chapati by using a rolling pin. (When cooked; these folds and the fat make the flaky layers in the paratha.)

Place the rolled paratha on the hot flat pan or a tawa. Using a suitable spoon spread ½-1 tablespoon of cooking oil all over the paratha and gently turn over the paratha using flat spatula and cook for 10-15 seconds. Repeat the application of the fat on other side and gently turn over the paratha again and cook this side of the paratha for further 10-15 seconds. Keep the paratha moving around the pan and keep flipping both sides using the tongs or spatula to avoid it burning. You will notice that the colour of the uncooked dough changes and small brown bubbles appear. If you notice that any part of the paratha is uncooked, just press it down with the spatula and continue to cook. Basically you need to cook each side for 30-40 seconds, but if you find it is not cooked properly just cook it for a longer time. If you prefer an extra crispy paratha then cook both sides on a very low heat for a longer time and spread extra fat over the paratha.

Serving suggestions:
Parathas are normally eaten with curries or egg omelettes or with lentils. But they are also good alternatives for making kebab rolls or making egg rolls with the omelette, or making jam rolls using a good quality jam of any type.

3.   Methi and spinach paratha

Serves 1-2

Ingredients:
50-100g wholemeal chapati flour
Handful of chopped spinach
Methi or coriander or water cress or chives
Small green chilli
Ground cumin
Salt
Butter or cooking oil

Method:
This is not a stuffed paratha because the filling is kneaded with the flour. The dough is prepared by adding the flour with chopped fresh spinach, methi fresh/dry leaves or fresh coriander if you cannot get hold of methi (fenugreek leaves), a small chopped green chilli or ½ teaspoon of red chilli powder, ½ a teaspoon of ground cumin and salt to taste. Mix everything well and knead the mixture using your hand or use a food processor. Use water in splashes to make firm smooth dough. Use recipe No: 2 of Chapter 5 for making plain paratha.

Serving suggestions:
You can eat the methi/spinach parathas as they are, but they also go well with plain yoghurt.

4.   4. Stuffed paratha

You can stuff the paratha with spiced mashed potatoes, mashed curried cauliflower, grated cheese, curried mincemeat, grated curried mooli or any vegetable or meat stuffing of your choice. You can make sweet paratha by using sugar or raisins instead of savoury stuffing.

Preparation of the different paratha filling/stuffing:

4a. Mashed potato paratha filling/stuffing:

Traditionally this is the most common and popular filling for parathas.

Mash 2 baked potatoes, add chilli, cumin, salt to taste to make a very simple stuffing. The addition of some fresh coriander or methi or spinach is optional.

On the other hand, you can use recipe No: 6 of Chapter 2, and add fresh coriander to make a good tasty potato stuffing. Or use recipe No: 21 of Chapter 2, the vegetable filling of the samosas.

4b. Mashed curried cauliflower filling/stuffing:

This is the second popular filling for parathas. Follow recipe No: 3 of Chapter 3C but make sure that the curry is as dry as possible, with minimum liquid or moisture. This will help in rolling the stuffed paratha. But recipes No: 1 and No: 7 of Chapter 3C all can be used as a paratha stuffing.

4c. Curried mincemeat stuffing:

Use recipe No: 21 of Chapter 2—the meat filling of the samosas. Or mincemeat with potato and peas curry (keema, Aloo and mutter) can be prepared. See recipe No: 14 of Chapter 3B.

4d. Grated curried mooli (Indian white radish) stuffing:

Peel, wash and grate two mooli. Take a suitable pan with 2 tablespoons of cooking oil and put it on the hob and add a teaspoon of cumin seeds. When the seeds start to pop, take it off the heat and add ½ a teaspoon of chilli powder, ¼ of a teaspoon of turmeric, and salt to taste. Put it back on the heat and add the grated mooli. Stir to mix everything. Put the lid on the pan and continue to cook until the mooli is cooked and all the liquid is dried. Let it cool to room temperature, then add fresh coriander and your mooli filling is ready for making the stuffed parathas.

Preparation of the paratha using any of the above stuffing:

Serves 3-4

Ingredients:
75-150g wholemeal chapati flour
½ cup of water
Butter or cooking oil of your choice for frying

Method:
The easy way to make the paratha dough is to use a food processor (or by using your hands). Put the flour in the food processor and a ¼ cup of water to start with, and then keep adding splashes of water until the dough is soft and smooth. Take out the dough and knead it with your hands for 3-5 minutes. Cover it with cling film and leave it to rest in a cool place. While the dough is resting, put a flat pan or a tawa on the medium hot hob.

If you prefer to be consistent with the size of the paratha, divide the dough into equal portions. Take one portion and roll it into a ball between the palms of your hands. On the kitchen work surface sprinkle dry flour and roll the dough slightly thicker than chapatis. Put 2-3 tablespoons of the stuffing of your choice in the centre and fold in the left and the right side towards the centre. Brush little butter or fat on the folds and then fold the top and the bottom side towards the centre. This square shaped dough with stuffing is gently rolled as thin as possible, using a rolling pin making sure that the stuffing stays in the rolled dough. (When cooked; these folds and the fat make the flaky layers in the paratha.)

Place the rolled paratha on the hot flat pan or a tawa. Spread ½-1 tablespoon of cooking oil all over the paratha and gently turn over the paratha using flat spatula and cook for 10-15 seconds. Repeat the application of the fat on other side of the paratha and gently turn over the paratha again and cook this side of the paratha for further 10-15 seconds. Keep the paratha moving around the pan and keep flipping both sides using the tongs or spatula to avoid it burning. You will notice that the colour of the uncooked dough changes and small brown bubbles appear. If you notice that any part of the paratha is uncooked, just press it down with the spatula and continue to cook. Basically you need to cook each side for 30-40 seconds but if it is not cooked properly just cook it for a longer time. If you prefer an extra crispy paratha then cook both sides on a very low heat for a longer time and spread extra fat over the paratha.

Serving suggestions:
This paratha does not need any curry so it can be eaten with lemon or mixed pickle. It is delicious if you spread some plain yoghurt and make a paratha roll.

5.   Baysen Ki Roti

Serves 2-3

Ingredients:
80-100g of baysen flour (chickpea flour)
20-50g of wholemeal wheat flour or rice/ cornmeal
½ cup of water for making the dough
1 teaspoon of ground coriander
1 teaspoon of ground garam masala
1 teaspoon of fresh/ground ginger
½ teaspoon of chopped green chillies
½ teaspoon of ground red chilli
Handful of fresh coriander
Fresh methi leaves or finely chopped spinach leaves; 1-2 tablespoon
Salt to taste
Cooking oil of your choice

Method:
The easy way to make the dough is to use a food processor. Put the both the flours and all other ingredients in a food processor and add ¼ cup of water to start with and then keep adding small splashes of water as required, until the dough is smooth but firm. Take out the dough and knead it with your hands for 3-5 minutes then cover with cling film. Leave it to rest. While the dough is resting, put a flat pan or a tawa on a medium heat. Cook baysen ki roti like a chapati and butter it while it is the hot or you can cook it like a plain paratha.

Serving suggestions:
Baysen ki roti is savoury and does not need any curry so it can be eaten as it is or with some plain yoghurt. But it is delicious with lemon or mixed pickle.

6.   Naan bread

Serves 3-4

Ingredients:
300-400g plain flour
Hot water (100ml)
1 teaspoon of sugar
2 teaspoons dried active yeast
¼ teaspoon of salt
1 teaspoon of baking powder
2-3 tablespoons of olive oil or any fat of your choice
4-5 tablespoons of plain yoghurt
1 medium sized lightly whisked egg is optional

Method:
Put the hot water in a bowl. Add the sugar and yeast, stir and it leave it aside until the yeast has dissolved and the mixture is frothy. The easy way to make the naan dough is to use a food processor. Put the flour, the salt, baking powder, olive oil, plain yoghurt, egg and the yeast mixture in the food processor. (Add water only if the dough is still hard or dry). Add splashes of water until the dough is smooth and firm, firmer than the chapati dough (make sure the dough is not as soft as the chapati dough). Take out the dough and knead it with your hands for 3-5 minute or so.

Cover with cling film. Leave it to rest for 1 hour so that the dough can rise. While the dough is resting and rising, put a flat pan or a tawa on the medium hot hob and preheat the grill.

If you prefer to be consistent with the size of the naans; then divide the dough into equal portions. Take one portion and roll between the palms of your hands. Then on a work surface, using dry flour, gently roll the dough roughly ½ inch thick by using a rolling pin or by using your hands. You can shape the dough by gently pulling it into either oblong or tear-shape naan.

We are cooking one side of the naan on the flat pan and the top side of the naan under the grill. Place the rolled naan on the medium hot flat pan and make sure that this side is well cooked. Using suitable tongs or spatula transfer the naan on the baking tray and place it under the grill to cook the top side. The naan will puff slightly and when golden-brown, remove from the grill. Keep the cooked naans in a bread cloth or a tea towel while you make the rest of the naans.

Serving suggestions:
Naans are served with all types of curries.

7.   Poories

Serves 1-2

Ingredients:
25-75g of plain or wholemeal flour
1 tablespoon of plain yoghurt
Pinch of salt
Cooking oil for deep frying the poories

Method:
The easy way to make the poori dough is to use a food processor. Put all the ingredients into a food processor. Mix without water and then add splashes of water until the dough is smooth and firm. Take the dough out and knead with your hands for 3-5 minutes. Cover with cling film and leave the pastry in the fridge at least for 30 minutes.

If using the electric deep fryer, then put it on a fairly hot setting, alternatively you can use a deep frying pan.

If you prefer to be consistent with the size of the poories, divide the dough into equal small portions. Take one portion and roll it between the palms of your hands and using a work surface sprinkle some dry flour and roll the dough out as thin as the chapati by using a rolling pin. Roll all the poories and then fry them one by one by placing the rolled poori into the hot fryer. The poories puff/ pop like a balloon. Cook it for 7-8 seconds each side. When it becomes light brown in colour it is cooked. Take the poories out of the hot fat and leave to drain on a paper towel

Serving suggestions:
Traditionally the poories are eaten with chickpea and potato dishes or with the semolina halva. They can also be eaten with all vegetable or meat curries, pickles, chutneys, yoghurt and with any of the halvas.

8. Pooray (pancakes)

Prooay bread:

Pancakes are made and consumed worldwide, under different names with many variations in the toppings and the fillings, and served at different times of the day, for special events and for the traditional occasions, too.

Chapati/paratha is also a sort of unleavened pancake made with wheat flour and water and is eaten with all savoury/sweet dishes. In contrast, naan bread is leavened thick pancake made with wheat flour and water and is eaten with all savoury dishes.

Both pooray and dosa are thin and crispy types of pancake breads. These are made from the batter which is leavened either with baking soda/baking powder or yeast or naturally fermented.

Using pooray and dosa widens the choice of bread to be eaten with meat and vegetable curries and also with some sweet dishes.

The basic recipe for making plain pooray (pancakes):

Ingredients:
125g of plain flour
2 eggs
Pinch of salt
¼ teaspoon of baking soda or baking powder
250ml of semi-skimmed milk
Butter/cooking oil for frying

Method:
Put all the ingredients in a suitable bowl and whisk to make a smooth thin batter.

***Note to remember:* Batter without egg is just as good, if preferred.**

How to make the pooray from the batter:

Heat the frying pan, melt a little butter/fat and pour about 30ml or 2 tablespoons of the batter. Rotate and tilt the pan to spread the batter evenly. Fry over a medium heat and when you see the bubbles appear and burst, and the edges of the pancakes start to dry, that is a good time to turn it over. Turn the pancake either by tossing it or simply flipping using a flat spatula. It takes about one minute to cook each side but make sure that both sides are golden-brown. Repeat the frying step of the pancakes until all the mixture is finished.

Serving suggestions:
There are many pancake toppings and fillings that can be used. In the west the most popular pancake toppings are lemon and sugar, jams, creams, peanut butter, fruit and ice-creams etc.

The aim of the pooray recipe is to give you more choice to eat the meat, vegetables and daal curries with. It is a good alternative of chapatti, paratha, naan bread or rice. But you can also make pooray sandwiches by using the filling in the pooray; fold it or roll it in any form or shape.

Note to remember: *Use the leftover curries, rice, and halvas as pancake toppings and fillings.*

Suggestions to create your own savoury and sweet fillings for pooray:

Create your own fillings by using recipes from Chapter 2, except recipes No: 22, 25 and 27. All the other twenty-four recipes are suitable to be eaten with the pooray.

From Chapter 3, all dry meat curries are suitable fillings; e.g. recipes No: 4, 5, 8, 14-16. But there is no reason why curries with sauce cannot be eaten with poorays. The same applies with vegetable dishes, recipes No: 1-8 and 10 are good fillings. But all lentils go very well with the Indian pancakes-pooray too.

Pooray/dosa can be used as wraps for all the meat/vegetable dishes from Chapters 2 and 3 with splashes of green chutneys, pickles and some green salad leaves.

The most suitable sweet fillings in Chapter 7 are the milk pudding and the halva recipes No: 2-4, but you can be creative and daring to try any other desserts as the filling.

The basic recipe for making savoury or sweet pooray (pancakes):

Prepare the batter by putting 125g of plain flour, 2 eggs, a pinch of salt and ¼ teaspoon of baking soda or baking powder and about 250ml of milk into a mixing bowl. To make sweet pooray, just add sugar to taste and whisk to make a smooth thin batter with the basic ingredients. This is a traditional and a popular way for Pakistani/Indians to enjoy poorays.

For the savoury pooray, add paneer, small amount of finely chopped onions, spinach with some chilli or black pepper, and salt to taste. Fry the savoury pooray as you normally fry the plain ones.

9. *Dosa bread is a crispy pancake made with rice and urid daal (with no wheat flour)*

Dosa is the staple food of the southern states of India, and is now eaten all over the world. It is very thin, crispy, round, fermented and gluten-free bread, traditionally made with rice and urid daal. The ratio of the rice to daal is 2:1; the amount of rice is twice the amount of the daal. Urid is the most common daal used, but chana and moong daal are good substitutes in the preparation of dosa. Wheat flour, semolina, maize or millet flour and baysen are the alternatives to rice. Dosa and baysen ki roti are gluten-free and could be a good choice for those with wheat intolerance

The authentic method of dosa preparation is slow and long, as the rice and urid daal are soaked in water (at least for 6 hours but preferably overnight) and then ground finely to make the batter. This batter of rice and daal is then fermented overnight in a warm part of your kitchen. At this stage you have the choice to add ingredients, like eggs, finely chopped vegetables, cheese and spices or sugar to make them sweet.

Healthy, quick and easy method to make the dosa batter:

In this microwave age, we are always looking for quick methods and so there is dosa-mix available and sold in shops. But we can even do a better job if we select our own ingredients to prepare a dosa-mix.

Ingredients:
1 cup of rice flour
½ cup of Urid or baysen flour
½ teaspoon baking powder or ¼ teaspoon of bicarbonate of soda

Method:
Put all the ingredients into a bowl and make a thin batter with water. Leave to rest.

How to make the Dosa from the batter:

Follow the instructions for how to make the pooray (pancakes) from the batter by using recipe No: 8 of this Chapter.

Serving suggestions:
Dosa is served hot with some butter or yoghurt chutney or green chutney, then rolled and eaten. It is traditionally used as a wrap for dry potato curry filling, and eaten with green coconut chutney. Dosa is also eaten with the daal curry, accompanied with pickles and chutneys.

Note to remember: Use the leftover dry curries, rice and halvas as dosa toppings and fillings.

Selection of the some suitable savoury and sweet fillings:

Create your own fillings by using the recipes from Chapter 2 (with the exception of recipes No: 22, 25 and 27). All the other twenty-four recipes are suitable as the topping and the filling for dosa, in one way or another.

From Chapter 3, all the dry meat curries are suitable fillings. E.g. recipes No: 4, 5, 8, and 14-16. But there is no reason why the curries with the runny sauce cannot be eaten with dosa.

The same applies with vegetable dishes, recipes No: 1 to 8 and No: 10 are good fillings. All the lentils are suitable to be eaten with the gluten-free crispy dosa bread.

Dosa can be used as wraps for all the rice dishes with splashes of green chutneys, pickles and some green salad leaves.

The most suitable sweet fillings in Chapter 7 are the milk pudding and the halva recipes No: 2-4, but you can be creative to try any other desserts as the filling.

Chapter 6

Indian Condiments

1. Pickles

There are so many different pickles to choose from. These are available from Indian stores and from most supermarkets. Lime, mango, garlic and green chilli pickle go really well with daal, meat, vegetables and all the rice dishes in this book. Chapatis and parathas are not always eaten with the curries but can be eaten just with pickles.

2. Hara Dhania chutney (Fresh coriander chutney)

Ingredients:
1 medium chopped onion
1 medium chopped tomato
Handful of fresh coriander
1 small green chopped chillies or as to taste
1 tablespoon anardana (dried pomegranate seeds washed and soaked in water; see recipe No: 11 of this Chapter) or 1 teaspoon of Imli paste (optional—but the tangy/sour taste of Imli works well in this chutney; see recipe No: 10 of this Chapter)
¼ teaspoon fresh grated ginger,
1 clove of garlic (if you like raw garlic)
¼ teaspoon of cumin powder
Salt to taste

Method:
Put all the ingredients into a blender and blend for 1-2 minutes to get a good smooth chutney sauce. Pour into a suitable small container with a lid and leave it in the fridge.

Also see recipe No: 11 of anardana (pomegranate seeds) chutney.

3.   Hara poodina chutney (Fresh mint chutney)

Ingredients:
1 medium chopped onion
1 medium chopped tomato
Handful of fresh mint
1 tablespoon anardana (dried pomegranate seeds washed and soaked in water; see recipe No: 11 of this Chapter) **or** 1 teaspoon of Imli paste (optional but the tangy and sweet taste of both Imli and anardana works well)
1 small green chopped chilli or as to taste
¼ teaspoon fresh grated ginger
¼ teaspoon of cumin powder
Salt to taste

Method:
Put all the ingredients into a blender and blend for 1-2 minutes to get a good smooth chutney sauce. Pour into a suitable small container with a lid and leave it in the fridge. Also see recipe No: 11 of anardana (pomegranate) chutney.

4.   Plain yoghurt with fresh chutneys

Take a cup of plain yoghurt and mix two tablespoons of either fresh coriander chutney or fresh mint chutney and mix well. Add salt to taste.

5.   Plain yoghurt and cucumber raita

Take a cup of plain yoghurt and add finely chopped cucumber and some finely chopped onion. Add salt and pepper to taste and a pinch of ground dry roasted cumin (small chopped green chilli is optional *but will add an extra appetising smell and taste*).

6. Plain yoghurt and potato or aubergine raita

Bake a small potato or a small aubergine, cut into small chunks and add to a cup of plain yoghurt. Season it with salt, pepper/red chilli powder or green chopped chilli. Finely chopped onions, tomato, fresh coriander and mint are optional. If the consistency of the raita is too thick, just add a little water.

Note to remember: Also see recipe 5, 7&8 of Chapter 2 for more raitas.

7. Plain yoghurt and boondi raita

Boondi is made from the baysen batter (chickpea flour) fried into tiny plain pakoras (they look like round beads) in vegetable oil and is normally sold in Indian shops. Boondi is one of the most popular raitas in Pakistan and India, served at weddings and other celebrations. It is a good condiment to serve with curries but it is especially popular with all the rice pulaos.

Ingredients and Method:
Take ½ cup of the boondi in a small sieve and pour some hot water to wash away extra fat and also to soften it. Mix it with 1 cup of plain yoghurt then add ¼ cup of water/milk to make the raita a bit runny because boondi absorbs a lot of liquid. As the boondi has no added flavour, add chilli powder or chopped green chilli, salt, and sprinkle ground dry roasted cumin. You could also add some chopped onion or green coriander/mint or even a chopped tomato adds a great taste to this raita.

8. Onion, tomato, red or white radish and cucumber salsa

Ingredients:
1 medium onion
2 medium tomatoes
3-4 red radishes or 2^{inches} of white radish
2-3^{inches} of cucumber
Juice of 1 lemon
Salt and pepper or green chilli

Method:
Chop all the ingredients and put them into a bowl and add 1 tablespoon of freshly squeezed lemon juice. Add salt and pepper or ½ a chopped green

chilli and mix all the ingredients thoroughly. This goes well with all the curries, the savoury rice dishes, the chapati wraps and the paratha/pancake/dosa rolls.

9. Plain yoghurt

Plain yoghurt (dahi) is the most common, popular, useful and nutritious accompaniment or condiment used with all curries, rice dishes and Indian breads and with most of the Indian savoury snacks.

10. Imli (Tamarind) chutney

Imli (Tamarind) pod is the fruit with the hard brown shell, and the soft edible pulp with flattened glossy brown seeds. The ripened pulp is sweet and sour, high in acid, vitamin B and calcium. Tamarind is widely used all over the world. Tamarind paste is blended into juices to make soft drinks. In the west this paste is used in the preparation of making many brown sauces. In Pakistan/India it is used in some lentils, vegetables and chaart recipes but it commonly used all over Pakistan and India in making the Imli chutney. Imli chutney goes well with most of the Indian snacks and with some curries. Imli water *(Tamarind paste diluted in water)* is an exotic alternative to the lemon juice.

Tamarind is sold in supermarkets in the form of a paste, ready to be used. But in the Indian stores it is commonly sold in blocks of shelled and deseeded pods with the moist pulp entangled in stringy fibres. The pulp is then extracted and made into the tamarind paste at home.

How to make your own tamarind paste:

Break the block into small pieces and soak in hot water for 30-40 minutes to soften and to loosen the flesh. Using your hands, squash and squeeze the pulp from the fibres; it comes off easily. Pass through a sieve to get rid of all the fibres or the seeds. Reduce the water from the tamarind pulp by using the hob (medium heat) until you get the consistency of a paste. This paste is used in making chutneys, in fact if you want to give any curry or chutney or chaart a sweet and tangy flavour, just add some tamarind paste or tamarind water.

How to make Imli Ki chutney:

Ingredients:
100g of tamarind paste
2 tablespoons of brown soft sugar (or as to taste)
½ cup of water
Salt /black salt to taste
¼ teaspoon of red chilli
½ teaspoon of roasted cumin powder
4-6 finely chopped mint leaves for extra flavouring or 1 tablespoon of finely chopped fresh coriander

Method:
Put all the ingredients (except the water) into a suitable bowl. Gradually add the water to mix all the ingredients to get a smooth chutney sauce and leave it in the fridge.

Serving suggestions: This chutney is sweet, sour and spicy, which goes especially well with the snacks and the starters of Chapter 2. It is good accompaniment for the daal and the rice dishes

11. Anardana (pomegranate seeds) chutney

Anardana is the dried seeds of one of the varieties of pomegranates, and they are very sour to eat as fresh fruit. The seeds are either sold whole or in the form of powder in the Indian food stores. It is mainly used in the preparation of chutneys, pakoras, potato, chickpeas and vegetable dishes.

Ingredients:
½ cup Anardana
Handful of fresh coriander is optional
½ cup of fresh mint leaves
1 large onion
1 medium tomato
1 small green chilli
1 teaspoon of grated ginger
Salt to taste

Method:

Wash the Anardana in a sieve under a running tap and soak it overnight for the best results. Alternatively soak the Anardana in hot water at least for an hour or so. Using a blender; grind the soaked seeds first; then add all other ingredients and grind to make a smooth chutney sauce. Pour into a suitable container and leave it in the fridge.

Note to remember: *Please go through the recipes cautiously to check if you are sensitive or intolerant to any of the ingredients and make sure to eliminate or to use a suitable alternative.*

Chapter 7

Indian Desserts:

I have divided the Indian desserts into 3 sections; the popular milk puddings, the well-known halvas and a large selection of mithai (Indian sweet meat).

Note to remember: Please go through the recipes cautiously to check if you are sensitive or intolerant to any of the ingredients and make sure to eliminate or to use a suitable alternative.

7A. Milk puddings

1.   Chawal Kheer (Rice pudding)

Rice pudding like the meatballs and pancakes is a universal dish. Rice and milk are the common ingredients. The method of cooking and the flavourings may vary from country to country. In Indian and Pakistan it is prepared as a dessert, as a festival food and also as a special food to treat children. This kheer is cooked by everyone but not everyone can afford to use expensive nuts and dried fruits. In fact creamy kheer slowly cooked with lots of cardamom flavoured milk is simply delicious and needs nothing more. But addition of anything else makes the dish very special.

Serves 3-4

Ingredients:
1 cup of broken rice or short-grain rice (basmati can be used)
1½ litres of whole or semi skimmed milk

Crushed seeds of 3-4 green cardamoms
1 clove for extra flavour
½ teaspoon of ground fennel
1^{inch} of cinnamon stick or ¼ teaspoon of cinnamon powder
¼-½ cup of unrefined sugar (remember that the raisins and the dates are adding some sweetness too)
Handful of raisins or sultanas
1 tablespoon of ground almonds
4-6 chopped soft dates
1 tablespoon of desiccated coconut (or sliced dry or fresh coconut)
1-2 teaspoons of rose water (optional)
Chopped pistachios and of sliced almonds for garnishing (handful)

Method:
Wash the rice in a sieve under running tap water. Soak the washed rice in warm water for at least 30 minutes. In a suitable saucepan add just over a litre of milk and leave the rest of the milk as a reserve in case you need it later if the rice pudding gets too thick. Bring the milk to the boil with the spices and then add the soaked rice and the desiccated coconut. Lower the heat and keep cooking and stirring occasionally until the rice is cooked. At this stage add the ground almonds, sugar and the raisins. Continue to cook and stir until the mixture is very creamy and does not stick to the spoon, but drops easily from the spoon.

How to the check the consistency of the pudding—by the drop test:

If the pudding sticks to the spoon and does not drop off easily, this means that its consistency is too thick. If that is the case, just gradually add more milk and stir until it passes the test.

Remove from the heat and transfer the rice pudding into the serving bowl and take out the cinnamon stick (not edible). Add a few drops of rose water or a few drops of saffron water (if preferred) and mix thoroughly into the pudding. Dry toast the almond slices and spread these with the chopped pistachios over the rice pudding. Sprinkle some dark chocolate shavings over the pudding if you are not fond of nuts or suffer with nut intolerance.

Serving suggestions:
Serve as a pudding after lunch or after the evening meal. It could be a good breakfast alternative to cereals with milk. It can be served hot or cold. It is served on special religious festivals.

2. Gujrella Kheer (Rice pudding with carrots)

This is a creamy rice pudding cooked with grated carrots. Like Gaajer (carrot) halva; the Gujrella is a winter dessert in Pakistan. The carrot really works well in this kheer, once it is tried, it could be your regular dessert

Serves 3-4

Ingredients:
1 cup of broken rice or short-grain rice (basmati can also be used)
2-3 medium grated carrots
1½ litres of whole or semi skimmed milk
Crushed seeds of 3-4 green cardamoms
½ teaspoon of ground fennel (optional)
1 ^{inch} of cinnamon stick or ½ teaspoon of cinnamon powder
¼-½ cup of unrefined sugar (remember that the carrots are adding some sweetness too)
Handful of raisins or sultanas
1 tablespoon of ground almonds
1 tablespoon of desiccated coconut (or sliced dry or fresh coconut)
1-2 teaspoon of rose water or saffron water is optional
Chopped pistachios and sliced almonds for garnishing (handful)

Method:
Wash the rice in the sieve under running tap water. Soak the washed rice in fairly warm water for at least 30 minutes. In a suitable saucepan pan add just over a litre of milk and leave the rest of the milk as a reserve in case you need it later if the rice pudding gets too thick. Bring the milk to the boil with the spices and then add the soaked rice, the grated carrots and the desiccated coconut. Lower the heat and keep cooking and stirring occasionally until the rice has swelled and the carrots are cooked. Add the ground almonds, sugar and the raisins and continue to cook and stir until the mixture is very creamy and does not stick to the spoon.

How to the check the consistency of the pudding is very easy—by the drop test:

If the pudding sticks to the spoon and does not drop off easily, this means that its consistency is too thick. If this is the case just gradually add more milk and stir until it passes the test

Remove from the heat and transfer the gajrella pudding into the serving bowl and take out the cinnamon stick (not edible). Add a few drops of rose water or a few drops of saffron water (if preferred). Mix thoroughly into the pudding. Dry toast the almond slices and spread these with the chopped pistachios over the gajrella pudding. Sprinkle some dark chocolate shavings over the pudding if you are not fond of nuts or suffer with nut intolerance.

Serving suggestions:
Serve as a pudding after lunch or after the evening meal. It could be a good breakfast alternative to cereals with milk. It can be served hot or cold.

3.   Phirini (Ground rice and milk pudding)

Serves 4-6

Ingredients:
¾ cup of rice flour
1½ litres of whole or semi skimmed milk
Crushed seeds of 3-4 green cardamoms
1 clove for extra flavour
3-4 strands of saffron, dissolved in a few spoons of hot milk
¼ cup of unrefined sugar (to add or reduce sugar according to your taste)
Handful of sliced almonds
1 tablespoon of ground almonds
Chopped pistachios
1-2 teaspoons of rose water (optional)

Method:
In a bowl put the rice flour and mix it with water to make a light and thin paste and leave it for 20-30 minutes

In a suitable saucepan add just over a litre of milk and leave the rest of the milk as a reserve in case you need it later if the Phirini gets too thick. Bring the milk with the spices to the boil and simmer for at least 10-20 minutes so that the spices will release their flavour and the milk will thicken. Then add the rice flour paste into the milk and continue to cook on a very low heat and keep stirring. Stir in the ground almonds and sugar. *Continue to cook and stir until the mixture coats the back of the cooking spoon*, but make sure that all the small grains of the ground rice are cooked. Remove from the heat and transfer the Phirini into the serving bowl. Add the rose water or saffron water if preferred. Mix thoroughly into the pudding. Dry toast the almond slices and spread these with chopped pistachios; over the rice pudding. Sprinkle some dark chocolate shavings over the pudding if you are not fond of nuts or suffer with nut intolerance.

Allow to cool then put it in the fridge to set. It should set nicely like a jelly.

Traditionally, Phirini is set in individual unglazed small earthenware serving plates or in an unglazed main serving earthenware dish.

Note to remember: Phirini takes much less time than the Chawal kheer (rice pudding)

Serving suggestions:
Serve as a pudding after lunch or after the evening meal. It could be a good breakfast, an alternative to cereals with milk. Traditionally it is served cold.

4.   Coconut Burfi

Serves 2-3

Burfi is a common and a popular Indian sweet, which is simply made from milk and sugar. Both ingredients are cooked until a semisolid-to-fudge like consistency. The different types of burfies get their names from what you add to the plain burfi. For example, if you add badams (almonds) it is known as Badam burfi. Pista burfi has added pistachios and Kaju burfi is made with added cashews. If you don't like nuts or intolerant to nuts, use chocolate, carrots or figs to make the burfi.

Ingredients:
100g of desiccated coconut
500ml of semi-skimmed milk or 200ml tin of evaporated milk
Crushed seeds of 1 green cardamom (optional)
20-30g of sugar (add more or less to your taste)
Butter for lining the tray

Method:
In a suitable pan put all the ingredients and put it on a medium heat. Keep cooking and stirring until all the liquid dries up. Take it off from the heat and line a cold tray with some butter. Pour and spread the mixture into the tray, gently press it down and let it set. Cut into oblong or kite shape pieces with a knife.

Serving suggestions:
A piece of burfi with a cup of tea or coffee is a good alternative to a biscuit, and any of the burfies can be eaten as healthy sweets. Using the same recipe you will be able to make the other burfies too.

5. Rasgullas and Rusmali (paneer dessert)

Rasgullas—is a delicate, light and healthy dessert made with homemade cheese and very light and flavoured sugar syrup. Rusmali is Rasgullas served in flavoured milk of a thick consistency and with ground pistachios or almonds.

Rasgullas (paneer dessert):

Serves: 2-3

To make the paneer for the Rasgullas, use recipe No: 26 of Chapter 2. The fluffy cheese is kneaded or rolled using hands as you do in dough making until it is smooth and pliable. Divide it into 6-8 portions and roll each portion into small smooth ball using the palm of your hands. Ensure there are no cracks. Then slightly flatten these balls with your fingers.

How to prepare the light sugar syrup:

Ingredients:
½-¾ cup of sugar
2-2¼ cup of water
Small pinch of ground or crushed green cardamom or use 2-3 strands of saffron

Method:
Use a saucepan with tight lid. Put in all the ingredients and bring it to the boil. Make sure that the sugar is dissolved. Add the Rasgullas and cover the pan with the lid. Boil for at least 3-4 minutes then reduce the heat and simmer for another 5 minutes. Rasgullas when cooked; doubles in size, and when gently pressed and released the spongy ball bounces back to the original shape. When cooked, transfer to a serving dish, cool it and leave it in the fridge to chill.

Serving suggestions:
Always serve the Rasgullas with the syrup, as the spongy balls have no added sweetness so the dessert needs to have the light sugar syrup.

Rusmali (paneer dessert):

Rusmali is when the Rasgullas are served in flavoured milk of a thick consistency and with ground pistachios or almonds.

How to prepare rabri—the thick flavoured milk for the Rusmali:

Before you prepare the milk sauce for the Rusmali, you need to make the Rasgullas first, using the above recipe No: 5

Ingredients:
250-300ml semi-skimmed milk
Crushed seeds of one cardamom
Saffron water (made with 1-2 strands of saffron with 1 tablespoon of water)
Rose water, just a small splash (optional)
1 tablespoon ground/crushed almonds or pistachios
Sugar to taste (remember that Rasgullas are soaked in light sugar syrup)

Method:
Make the Rasgullas first by using the above recipe for the Rasgullas in the light sugar syrup. Put all the ingredients in a suitable pan. On a medium heat, reduce the milk to a thick consistency, while stirring several times to avoid the milk sticking/burning at the bottom. Carefully take out the Rasgullas from the syrup and add to the prepared milk mixture, add the saffron and put the lid back and simmer for 5 minutes on a very low heat. Transfer into a serving dish, cool it and leave in the fridge to chill. Garnish with some extra nuts or some shavings of dark chocolate.

Serving suggestions:
Traditionally Rusmali is served on all celebrations, parties and weddings but as a dessert it can be eaten with any meal.

6.   Savayian kheer (Fine vermicelli noodles pudding)

Serves 3-4

Ingredients:
2-3 cups of vermicelli (break the long fine or any other variety of vermicelli into small pieces and dry roast or roast in 1 tablespoon of butter or any cooking fat until light brown. Alternatively, buy the pre-roasted packs of vermicelli.
500-700ml of whole or semi-skimmed milk
Crushed seeds of 2-3 green cardamoms
1 clove for extra flavour
Saffron water (made with 1-2 strands of saffron with 1 tablespoon of water)
Or rose water, just a small splash
1 teaspoon of desiccated coconut
2 tablespoons of unrefined sugar (remember that the raisins and the dates are adding some sweetness too)
1 tablespoon of ground almonds
3-4 small chopped dates
Handful of raisins or sultanas
1 tablespoon of pumpkin or melon seeds (optional)
1 teaspoon of crushed poppy seeds (optional)
Chopped pistachios and 5-10g of sliced almonds for garnishing

Method:
Pour 500-600ml of milk into a suitable saucepan with the crushed green cardamoms, the desiccated coconut, chopped dates and the ground almonds and bring to the boil, then reduce the heat and on a medium heat keep stirring for 3-4 minutes. Add the roasted vermicelli, raisins or sultanas, the sugar and keep stirring until the vermicelli is cooked. It is entirely up to you whether you make it into a creamy texture like the rice pudding or a bit thinner. Both taste good. Traditionally its consistency is much thinner than the rice kheer. Remove from the heat and transfer into a serving bowl. Add the rose water or saffron and mix thoroughly into the pudding. Dry toast the almond slices and spread these with the chopped pistachios over the pudding. Sprinkle some dark chocolate shavings over the pudding. Allow to cool then put it in the fridge to set. It is a refreshing cold dessert in the summer.

Serving suggestions:
Serve as a pudding after lunch or after the evening meal. It could be a good breakfast, an alternative to cereals with milk. Savayian kheer or Savayian halva is served hot or cold on the religious festivals in Pakistan and India.

7.   Shahi Tokraay (Bread Pudding)

Serves 3-4

Ingredients:
1 litre of whole or semi-skimmed milk
5-7 slices of bread
Crushed seeds of 2-3 green cardamoms
Sugar (unrefined) about ¼ cup or add more if preferred
1 tablespoon of ground almonds
Chopped pistachios
Handful of raisin or sultanas
Pinch of nutmeg and cinnamon
60-100g of butter to fry the bread
1 large egg or 2 small eggs (slightly whisked)
Sliced almonds (for garnishing)

Method:

To make the 4 triangular pieces cut each slice of the bread diagonally. Fry the bread golden-brown using the butter in a frying pan. Drain them on the paper towel. If you want to use less fat, toast the bread in a toaster and slightly butter both sides. Line an oven dish with some butter and arrange the fried bread in the dish. Scatter the raisins/sultanas over the fried bread.

In a suitable pan put the milk, the sugar, the ground almonds, the nutmeg, the cinnamon, the crushed cardamoms and the chopped pistachios. Heat the pan over a medium-high heat for 5-10 minutes, to dissolve the sugar and to let the spices release their flavours, and don't forget to frequently stir the milk. Let it cool and then pour it over the whisked egg and mix it thoroughly. Pour this egg and milk mixture over the fried bread and sprinkle the sliced almonds on top and put it in a preheated oven at 180°C/355°F/ Gas 4 for 20-30 minutes (adjust the time according to your oven, the fan heated electric oven can take less time) or until the egg and milk mixture has set and the top is golden-brown. Take it out of the oven, let it rest for 10 minutes and serve.

Alternative method:

If you wish to eliminate the use of egg from the recipe and go for a lighter version of the pudding. All you have to do is to thicken the milk little bit more on the hob and reduce the volume of the milk to half. Line an oven dish with some butter and arrange the fried bread in the dish, scatter the raisins/sultanas and the chopped pistachios over the fried bread. Pour the reduced milk over the fried bread and sprinkle the sliced almonds on top. Put it in a preheated oven for 15-20 minutes at 180°C/355°F/Gas 4. Make sure that the pudding doesn't get too dry.

Serving suggestions:

Serve as a pudding after lunch or after the evening meal. It could be a good breakfast, an alternative to cereals with milk. It can be served hot or cold.

8.   Pista (pistachio) or mango Kulfi (Indian ice cream)

Serves 3-4

Ingredients:
1 litre of whole milk
Seeds of 2-3 green cardamoms, crushed as fine as possible
¼ cup of unrefined sugar
¼ cup of finely chopped pistachios
Few strands of saffron (optional)
Flakes of almond or chocolate shavings for garnishing

Method:
In a suitable saucepan add the milk, the crushed cardamom seeds and the strands of saffron. Bring it to the boil and then reduce the heat and simmer until the milk is reduced roughly to one third of the original volume of the milk (when one litre of milk is reduced to almost 320-330ml). Take the pan off the heat and dissolve the sugar and then add the finely chopped pistachios. Pour the mixture in a container with a lid and let it cool. Place it in the freezer until the mixture sets. Take the Kulfi out of the freezer about 5-7 minutes before serving.

Serving suggestions:
Serve the Kulfi as it is or garnish with flakes of almonds or chocolate shavings. Kulfi is everyone's favourite dessert in the hot summer.

9.   Yoghurt as a dessert
The most nutritious, inexpensive, simple and easiest healthy dessert is plain yoghurt in a bowl with unrefined sugar, or a spoon of jam or marmalade or some chopped fresh fruit. Yoghurt with chopped fruit can be frozen to a make it a healthy and delicious ice dessert.

7B. Halva Desserts

1. Savayian (Vermicelli) halva

Serves 2-3

Ingredients:
2-3 cups of vermicelli (snapped into small pieces)
Crushed seeds of 2-3 green cardamoms
1 tablespoon of desiccated coconut
½-1 cup of unrefined sugar (to add or reduce sugar according to your taste)
1 tablespoon of ground almonds
Handful of raisins or sultanas
1 tablespoon of pumpkin or melon seeds (optional)
1 teaspoon of poppy seeds (optional)
1 tablespoon of ground almonds
Chopped pistachios for garnishing
Rose water or few strands of saffron
1-2 cups of warm water
Butter or fat of your choice, about 4-5 tablespoons

Method:
In a suitable saucepan melt the butter on low heat with the crushed seeds of the green cardamoms and stir for about 3-5 seconds. Then add the vermicelli, raisins and the nuts; stir until roasted to light brown and the raisins swell. Add the desiccated coconut, the ground almonds, and stir for another 3-4 seconds. Take it off the heat to add warm water and then the sugar and put it back on the heat. Keep stirring until the vermicelli is cooked on fairly high heat and all the water dries up. Take it off from the hob and transfer it into a serving bowl. It is optional but you could spread some more nuts on top.

Serving suggestions:
Serve as a pudding after lunch or after the evening meal. It could be a good breakfast, an alternative to cereals with hot milk. It is always served hot and goes well with a cup of tea. It is served on special religious festivals.

2. Semolina/Sooji halva

Serves 2-3

Ingredients:
1 cup of dry roasted semolina in a pan on medium heat, stirring to avoid
burning
Crushed seeds of 3-4 green cardamoms
½ teaspoon ground fennel
1 tablespoon of desiccated coconut
½ cup of unrefined sugar *(The traditional recipe uses 1:1 of semolina and sugar)*
1 tablespoon of ground almonds
Handful of raisins or sultanas
1 tablespoon of pumpkin/melon seeds
1 teaspoon of poppy seeds (optional)
Chopped pistachios and some sliced almonds for garnishing
Rose water or few strands of saffron
2 cups of hot water
Butter or fat of your choice, about 3-4 tablespoons

Method:
Boil the 2 cups of water with the sugar, the fennel and seeds of the green
cardamoms, for 2-3 minutes to get their full flavours and to dissolve the
sugar.

In a suitable saucepan melt the butter on a low heat with the raisins and
the nuts. Stir until the raisins swell and then add the desiccated coconut,
the ground almonds, and the dry roasted semolina. Take it off the heat and
add the sugary and flavoured water (prepared earlier). Put the saucepan
back on the heat, keep stirring until the semolina swells and every grain is
cooked. It is important to make sure that all the water dries up completely.
This gives a good texture to the halva. Right at the end add a few drops of
rose water/saffron and mix into the halva. Take it off the heat and transfer
into a serving bowl. It is optional if you want to spread some more nuts on
the top; or take it off the heat and line a cold tray with some butter. Pour
and spread the halva in the tray. Gently press it down and let it set. Cut
into oblong or kite shape pieces with a knife.

Note to remember for all the halva preparations: Butter adds good taste, but if you want to cut down on butter, I would suggest you to use a cooking oil of your choice and add just a tablespoon of butter for flavour. Good halva is fluffy and moist; not gluey with too much moisture. If your halva is sticky and gluey, add one more spoon of fat and on a low heat keep cooking and stirring until it is fluffy and most of the liquid is dried.

Serving suggestions:
It is served hot and goes well with a cup of tea. Semolina halva is eaten with or without the poories during special festivals. To make poories, see recipe No: 7 of Chapter 5. It can be a good filling for the pooray and the dosa bread; see recipes No: 8 and No: 9 of Chapter 5.

It is served on special religious festivals.

3.   Baysen and egg halva

Serves 3-4

Ingredients:
1 cup of chickpea flour
Crushed seeds of 3-4 green cardamoms
1 teaspoon ground fennel
1 tablespoon of desiccated coconut
½ cup of unrefined sugar (to add or reduce sugar according to your taste)
Handful of raisins or sultanas
1 tablespoon of pumpkin or melon seeds
1 teaspoon of poppy seeds is optional)
1 tablespoon of ground almonds
Chopped pistachios for garnishing
1 whisked egg
Rose water or few strands of saffron is optional
1 cup of hot water
Butter or fat of your choice, about 3-4 tablespoons

Method:
Boil the water with the sugar, the fennel and seeds of the green cardamoms for 2-3 minutes to get their full flavours and to dissolve the sugar. In a suitable saucepan melt the butter on a low heat with the raisins and the

nuts. Stir until the raisins swell and the then add the desiccated coconut, the ground almonds and the chickpea flour, and stir until the flour is light brown. Take it off the heat to cool a little and then add the sugary flavoured water (prepared earlier). Put the saucepan back on the heat. Keep stirring until the chickpea flour swells and all the water dries up. Take it off the heat again and let it cool (from hot to warm) and then add some of the whisked egg and keep on stirring and mixing the egg, until you have poured in all the egg. Put it back on a low heat until the egg is cooked and then add a few drops of rose water/saffron and mix into the halva. If the halva looks too dry or gluey then add a tablespoon of the fat and keep it on the heat and keep stirring until all moisture dries up. Take it off the heat and transfer it into a serving bowl. It is optional to spread some more nuts on the top; or take it off the heat and line a cold tray with some butter and spread the halva in the tray. Gently press it down and let it set. Cut into oblong or kite shape pieces with a knife.

Serving suggestions:
It is always served hot and goes well with a cup of tea. The baysen halva is eaten with or without poories, pooray and dosa. It is considered by many Pakistani/Indians that this halva is one of the cures for the common cold. Even so, consuming Baysen and egg halva is a delicious and nutritious treat.

4. Gaajer (carrot) halva

Serves 3-4

Ingredients:
1 Kg of peeled and grated carrots
700-800ml of whole or semi-skimmed milk or 200g tin of evaporated milk
Crushed seeds of 2-3 green cardamoms
1 tablespoons of desiccated coconut (for the coconut lovers)
½ cup of unrefined sugar (to add or reduce sugar according to your taste)
1 tablespoon of ground almonds
Handful of raisins or sultanas
1 tablespoon of pumpkin/melon seeds
Chopped pistachios for garnishing
Just enough butter to roast raisins and pistachios (½-1 tablespoon)

Method:

In a suitable saucepan put the milk, the crushed cardamoms seeds, the grated carrots, ground almonds and the desiccated coconut. Bring to the boil and then reduce the heat, add the sugar and keep cooking and stirring until the carrots are cooked and all the liquid has dried up.

Melt the butter in a frying pan and add the raisins, the chopped nuts and stir until the nuts are roasted and the raisins swell. Take it off the heat and pour it over the cooked carrot halva and mix the nuts and raisin into the halva. Transfer the halva into a serving dish or take it off the heat and line a cold tray with some butter and spread the halva in the tray. Gently press it down and let it set. Cut into oblong or kite shape pieces with a knife.

Serving suggestions:

It is always served hot and goes well with a cup of tea. It is a popular winter pudding and also served on special occasions. Cold halva is eaten as mithai (sweet meat).

5.   Baysen ladoo

Serves: 3-5

Ingredients:
2 cup of baysen
¼ cup of semolina or rice flour
½-¾ cup sugar
¼-½ cup of ghee/butter
¼ cup of finely chopped almonds, cashew nuts, and pistachios
Pinch of ground fennel

Method:

In a suitable saucepan melt the butter on a low heat with a pinch of ground fennel and stir for about 3-5 seconds. Then add the baysen and the chopped nuts. Roast until you can smell the sweet aroma of the roasted baysen. Baysen burns very quickly, therefore you need to stir the mixture continuously on a very low heat. Take it off the heat and *cool it from hot to warm.* Add sugar and mix thoroughly. Take a handful of the mixture in your hand and squeeze gently to bind the mixture together and then roll into a ladoo (ball). Alternatively, after adding the sugar and mixing thoroughly and spread the mixture in a tray, gently press it down and let it set. Cut into oblong or kite shape pieces with a knife.

Serving suggestions:
Baysen ladoos can be served as a snack or as a dessert with a cup of tea or coffee.

6.   Zarda rice (Yellow sweet rice)

This traditional wedding sweet dish gets its name from the Urdu word, *zarid* which means yellow. The rice is prepared with yellow food colour, light or dark shade of yellow depends on how much food colour is used.

Serves 2-3

Ingredients:
1 cups of good basmati rice, washed and soaked in warm water
Crushed seeds of 2-3 green cardamoms
1 tablespoons of desiccated coconut or small slices of coconut
¾ cup of unrefined sugar (Traditional recipe uses rice: sugar 1:1 or even 1:2 but we can reduce sugar according to our need and taste.)
1 tablespoon of citrus peels dried or fresh (orange) finely chopped
One pinch of saffron soaked in a tablespoon of hot milk/water
1-2 teaspoons of egg yellow food colour
20-25g of raisins or sultanas
20g of sliced almonds
Handful of chopped pistachios
¼ cup of fresh or tin cubes of pineapple (optional)
½ cup of water to dissolve the sugar
Butter or fat of your choice, about 3-4 tablespoons

Method:
In a saucepan add plenty of hot water. Add the seeds of 2-3 green cardamoms, the black cloves and the food colouring. Boil it for about 3-4 minutes to let the cardamoms and the black cloves to release their aromas and the flavours.

Drain the water from the soaking rice and add the rice to this flavoured water *and boil the rice for about 4 minutes* (note the colour of the rice while it's boiling; if too pale just add bit more food colour). *Pour the boiled rice into a colander and try to strain it quickly to avoid overcooking—the rice at this stage should be partially cooked.*

Melt the butter in a saucepan and roast the nuts, the coconut, the raisins/sultanas and the orange peels. Then add the saffron, ½ cup of water and the sugar and bring to the boil. Add the boiled yellow rice (and add the pineapple cubes) into the sugary mixture. Mix it gently to avoid breaking the rice grains. Simmer zarda rice 10-15 minutes or until the rice are cooked.

☺ *See the note on simmering techniques in Chapter 4.*

Serving suggestions:
It is traditionally a hot dessert served at weddings, special parties and religious celebrations. I still remember at the village weddings in Pakistan many people served the meat pulao rice and the sweet zarda rice on the same plate, in order to eat the sweet and the savoury rice together. Whereas some people enjoyed plain yoghurt with their sweet rice, many still prefer both the combinations.

7C. Mithai (Indian sweet meat)

There is a big variety of Indian sweet meats sold in the mithai shops and not many people feel confident to make them all at home.

Here is a list of the common ones and their main ingredients:

* Burfi plain or with nuts is made from milk, sugar and almonds or pistachios or cashew nuts or coconut. See milk pudding recipe No: 4 of Chapter 7A
* There are quite a few types of Ladoo but the main ingredients are chickpea flour, sugar, raisins and nuts. For baysen kay ladoo, see halva dessert recipe No: 5 of Chapter 7B
* Ja-labis are very sweet but delicious and crispy. They are made from plain flour, fat and thick sugar syrup
* Pittasa is a sweet which is delicately made with many thin layers—that melts in your mouth. It is cleverly made just from the chickpea flour, sugar and fat.

- ❖ Gulab jaman are made from powdered milk, thick sugar syrup and fat.
- ❖ Rasgullas, Rasmalai, are all made from sugar, nuts and paneer. See milk pudding recipe No: 5 of Chapter 7A
- ❖ Balooshahi is flaky and crispy—made from plain flour, fat and sugar
- ❖ Gaajer halva made at home is more or less the same as the one sold in the sweet shops. The ingredients are carrots, milk, sugar and nuts.

A box of the mithai is like a box of chocolates/sweets; a gift given and received from others. There is no wedding, birthday party or any other celebration without mithai. Mithai is the main item of celebration food.

Chapter 8

Homemade cold and hot beverages:

Besides tea and coffee, there are some other hot and cold drinks which can be easily and conveniently prepared at home. These are *common, non-alcoholic, caffeine-free, healthier, economical,* and *flavoursome* drinks that can be enjoyed. These drinks can be consumed at any time of the day, with or after the meal. The ones which are listed here are light and delicate drinks for you to enjoy.

Note to remember: *Please go through the recipes cautiously to check if you are sensitive or intolerant to any of the ingredients and make sure to eliminate or to use a suitable alternative.*

8A. Cold beverages

1. Plain water

Plain water is the best drink of all times as it is one of the essential categories of food. See Chapter 1 on 'Basics of food' for the vital role that water plays in our body.

2. Shikanjbi (Shikanjbeen/ Shikanjvi) or Leemoo paani (Fresh homemade Lemonade)

Ingredients:
Still or sparkling water
Juice of ½-1 fresh lemon or lime

Sugar to taste
Pinch of table salt/kala numick (black salt)

Method:
Dissolve sugar and a pinch of salt in a glass or about 200ml of water. Then add the juice of ½ fresh lemon and mix well. Add more lemon juice and sugar to your taste. Serve with few ice cubes or leave it in the fridge to chill the Shikanjbi.

3.   Mint cold tea

Ingredients:
2 cups of boiled water
7-10 leaves of fresh mint
Lemon juice for extra flavour
Sugar or honey or sweetener of your choice

Method:
Put the mint leaves in a big tumbler or in a small teapot and pour hot water from the kettle that is freshly boiled. Cover and steep for 3-4 minutes to get the maximum flavour from the mint leaves. Strain and leave to cool. Add ½ teaspoon of lemon for extra flavour and if preferred also add sugar or honey. Mix everything well. Serve with few cubes of ice. Any extra tea can be left it in the fridge.

4.   Lessee drink

See Chapter 2 on "Healthy Snacks and Starters", recipe No: 25.

5.   Imli (Tamarind) drink

Ingredients:
½-1 teaspoon of Imli paste (see recipe No: 10 of Chapter 6)
Lemon juice or mint for extra flavour
1 glass cold water
Sugar or honey or sweetener of your choice
Pinch of table salt/kala numick (black salt)

Method:
Mix all ingredients and adjust the sugar and the extra flavours to your own taste. Make it cold by adding few cubes of ice.

8B. Hot beverages

1.   Elaichi Chai (black tea delicately flavoured with green cardamom)

To make this tea, it doesn't matter which brand of black tea you choose, because you have selected the cardamom flavouring for your chai. There are two methods. Boil the water with the cardamom seeds in it and then make the tea as you usually would, but this time use the flavoured water. Or, make the tea by using the teabag with the fine cardamom powder.

Ingredients:
1 mug of water
Seeds of ½ cardamom or tip of a teaspoon of cardamom powder
Milk to taste
Sugar or honey or sweetener of your choice

Method:
Take a suitable pan and boil a full mug of water with 2-3 seeds of cardamom and boil the water for 2-3 minutes (boil for longer time if you prefer a stronger flavour). Strain the boiling water into a mug with a teabag and make the tea as you normally do, or make the tea by using the tea bag with the fine cardamom powder. Both tea and cardamom will brew and give their own flavours. Add milk and sugar to taste.

2.   Saunf chai (Fennel seeds tea)

Saunf (seeds) is one of the most common, inexpensive and extensively used spice in Pakistan and India. Fresh saunf is light green in colour, available in all Indian food shops and is sold in packs of all sizes. Fennel seeds as a condiment are chewed after the meal. This tradition in the Indo-Pakistan culture has been going for very long time. It is considered that saunf is good for digestion and refreshes the mouth. There are some exciting chewing mixtures which have been created with dry roasted saunf, small pieces of coconut, chopped almonds and small pieces of crystalline crunchy sugar (mishri). The seeds, either whole or ground, are used in curries, pickles, desserts and in making chai.

How to make the fennel tea powder:

A good cup of saunf chai is made by using roasted fennel seeds. Roasting of these seeds is very simple and takes 1-2 minutes. Dry roast the seeds in a frying pan on a medium heat, until the seeds are light brown and gives the saunf aroma. Cool them and grind to a fine powder. Store the fine ground fennel in an air tight jar.

Note to remember: The finer the powder is the quicker it gives out its maximum flavour and the faster it sinks and settles down as a residue. When sweetening your saunf chai, please keep in mind that fennel has a slight natural sweet flavour.

Ingredients:
< ¼-¼ teaspoon saunf powder
1 tea mug of boiling water
Sugar or honey or sweetener of your choice
Strainer with the fine mesh

Method:
Pour boiling water into a tea mug with the saunf powder. Stir well and leave for 25-30 seconds to get the flavour. *Long steeping is not required as the flavours are released very quickly,* unless you want a very strong tea.

The residue of the powder settles down very quickly to the bottom of the mug. You can either carefully decant the liquid into another mug or pass it through a strainer. Your third choice is to drink the saunf chai from the same mug and leave the sediment at the bottom.

Serving suggestions:
It is a refreshing, light and delicately flavoured hot drink; after a curry meal.

3. Fresh ginger root tea

Ginger root, turmeric root and cardamom pods are all members of the same plant family. They are widely used in Indian cooking. Both ginger and turmeric have a pungent smell and strong taste, whereas the cardamom has a sweet and delicate taste. Ginger is widely used in most of the Indian and the Chinese cooking and ginger root tea is consumed all over the world.

Ingredients:
¼ teaspoon peeled and crushed fresh ginger
1 teaspoon lemon juice
1 thin slice of any fruit (e.g. apple to balance the strong taste of ginger)
Sugar or honey or sweetener of your choice

Method:
Pour boiling water in a mug with the ginger and a slice of apple. Stir well and leave it for 25-30 seconds to get the right amount of flavour. Long steeping is not required as the flavours are released very quickly and the essential oils of the ginger can make the tea too strong to drink. Strain the drink and add lemon, and sweeten with honey or sugar.

Serving suggestions:
Good alternative to a hot cup of coffee or tea after a meal.

4. Masala (spiced) Chai (tea)

The ingredients that make the masala chai are cardamoms, cloves, cinnamon, the ginger, fennel seeds and black tealeaves. Teabags of masala chai are available in most food stores. The method to make this is the same as making ordinary tea, and can be served with or without milk, and sugar, honey or sweetener of your choice.

Note to remember: *I find one teabag of the masala chai very strong for one cup of tea. So I recommend do not brew it for too long or make two cups of tea from one teabag.*

5. Mint tea

Ingredients:
2 cups of boiled water
7-10 leaves of fresh mint leaves
Sugar or honey or sweetener of your choice
Lemon juice for extra flavour

Method:
Put the mint leaves in a big tumbler or in a small teapot and pour boiling water from the kettle that is freshly boiled. Cover and steep for 3-4 minutes (or steep for a shorter time for a lighter tea) to get the maximum flavour from the mint leaves. Add ½ teaspoon of lemon for extra flavour and if preferred, also add sugar or honey.

Serving suggestions:
It is a refreshing, light and delicately flavoured hot drink, after a curry meal.

6. Celery chai

I find this infusion the most refreshing and appealing, with a delicate flavour.

Ingredients:
1 tea mug of boiled water
2-3 fresh celery leaves (pieces of the celery stick can be used too)
Lemon juice for extra flavour
Sugar or honey or sweetener of your choice

Method:
Put the celery leaves in a big tumbler or in a small teapot and pour boiling water from a kettle that is freshly boiled. Cover and steep for 3-5 minutes to get the maximum flavour from the celery leaves. Add ½ teaspoon of lemon for extra flavour and if preferred you can also add sugar or honey.

Serving suggestions:
It is a refreshing, light and delicately flavoured hot drink, after a curry meal.

8C. Kanji (The naturally fermented carrot drink)

Kanji is a spicy and tangy fermented carrot drink, normally made with dark purple carrots and water, in earthen or stoneware.

Ingredients:
3-4 medium orangey-red carrots
2 litres of water
2 tablespoons of crushed mustard seeds

1-2 tablespoon of cooking salt or ¾ tablespoon of cooking salt and ¼ tablespoon of black salt
1 teaspoon of cayenne pepper

Method:
Peel and wash the carrots and cut them length wise, ¼ ^{inch} thick and 3-4 ^{inch} long.

In a suitable pan, boil the water and add all the ingredients and mix well. Switch off the heat, cover the pan and leave it to cool. It will be good if you can get an earthenware or stoneware jar, but a thoroughly clean glass/plastic jar with a lid would be fine. Transfer the contents (when it reaches room temperature) of the pan into a jar. Put the lid on and leave in a fairly warm part of your kitchen for 3-4 days. The colour of the fermented liquid gets darker, and will taste tangy and sharp. Strain the liquid and refrigerate the liquid in a jug and the pickled carrots in a container.

Serving suggestions:
Serve kanji any time of the day. It can be served before or after the meal. The carrots are pickled and can be used in a salad.

<u>Final Note to Remember:</u>
Preserve and treat food as you would your body, remembering that in time food will be your body. ~B.W. Richardson

Healthy Indian recipes—Ultimate cooking guide supports . . .

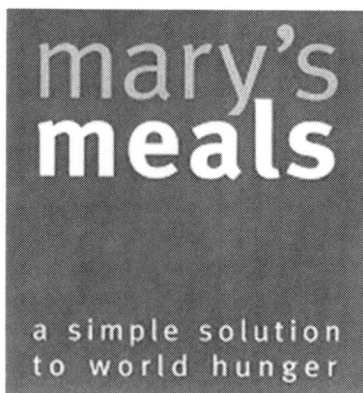

Mary's Meals is an international movement that sets up school feeding projects in communities where poverty and hunger prevent children from gaining education. Mary's Meals is a simple idea that works. By providing a daily meal in a place of education, chronically poor children are attracted to the classroom where they can gain a basic education that provides an escape route from poverty. Over 600,000 children receive Mary's Meals every school day. The average cost to feed a child for a whole school year is £10.70 (€12.40) ($16.80).

Big Blue Mug campaigns—fill a mug; feed a child with Mary's Meals for a year.

www.marysmeals.org.uk

Head Office:
Craig Lodge,
Dalmally, Argyll
PA33 1AR. UK
Registered Charity: SC022140
Limited Company: SC265941
Telephone: 00 44 (0) 1838 200605

www.marysmeals.org.
info@marysmeals.org
Facebook.com/marysmeals
Twitter.com/marysmeals
Vimeo.com/marysmeals
Youtube.com/marysmeals

MARY'S MEALS NEEDS YOUR SUPPORT!

Lightning Source UK Ltd.
Milton Keynes UK
UKOW050307060213

205884UK00002B/122/P